Pitt Press Series

The Story of the Kings
of Rome

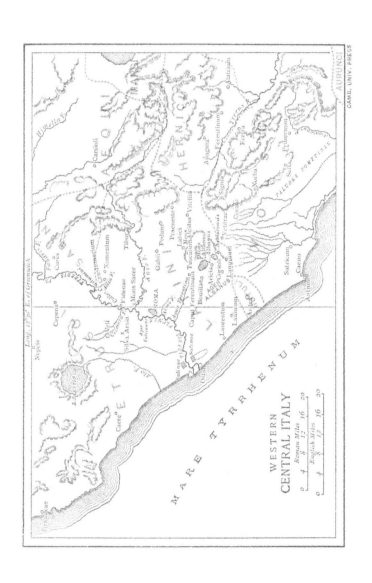

WESTERN
CENTRAL ITALY

Roman Miles
0   4   8   12   16   20

English Miles
0   4   8   12   16   20

The Story of the Kings of Rome

Adapted from Livy

With Notes and Vocabulary

by

G. M. Edwards, M.A.,
Fellow of Sidney Sussex College, Cambridge

Cambridge :
at the University Press
1914

CAMBRIDGE UNIVERSITY PRESS
Cambridge, New York, Melbourne, Madrid, Cape Town,
Singapore, São Paulo, Delhi, Tokyo, Mexico City

Cambridge University Press
The Edinburgh Building, Cambridge CB2 8RU, UK

Published in the United States of America by Cambridge University Press, New York

www.cambridge.org
Information on this title: www.cambridge.org/9781107620612

First published 1903
Reprinted 1904, 1911, 1914
First paperback edition 2011

A catalogue record for this publication is available from the British Library

ISBN 978-1-107-62061-2 Paperback

PREFACE.

THESE stories from the First Book of Livy have
been considerably simplified, especially in the
earlier chapters. In the latter part of the book,
where fewer alterations have been made, the
beauty and vigour of Livy's style have not, I
trust, been altogether spoilt by my editing. My
text, though simple and straightforward, will be
found to contain a large amount of useful Latin
idiom.

G. M. E.

July 15, 1903.

CONTENTS.

INTRODUCTION.

THAT we may understand the character of the stories of early Rome, it will be well to consider the full record of a single reign. The story of Numa, the second king, may be selected for this purpose.

Let me quote the beautiful version of it, which Dr Arnold, in his History of Rome, has put together from Livy and other writers :—

'When Romulus was taken from the earth, there was no one found to reign in his place. The Romans and the Sabines each wished that the king should be one of them. At last it was agreed that the king should be a Sabine, but that the Romans should choose him. So they chose Numa Pompilius; for all men said that he was a just man, and wise, and holy. Before he would consent to be king, Numa consulted the gods by augury, to know whether it was their pleasure that he should reign. And, as he feared the gods at first, so did he even to the last. He appointed many to minister in sacred things, such

as the Pontifices, who were to see that all things
relating to the gods were duly observed by all;
and the Augurs, who taught men the pleasure of
the gods concerning things to come; and the
Flamens, who ministered in the temples; and the
Virgins of Vesta, who tended the ever-burning fire;
and the Salii, who honoured the god of arms with
solemn songs and dances through the city on
certain days, and who kept the sacred shield which
fell down from heaven.

'And in all that he did Numa knew that he
would please the gods; for he did everything by
the direction of the nymph Egeria, who honoured
him so much that she took him to be her husband,
and taught him in her sacred grove, by the spring
that welled out from the rock, all that he was to
do towards the gods and towards men. By her
counsel he snared the gods Picus and Faunus in
the grove on the Aventine hill, and made them
tell him how he might learn from Jupiter the
knowledge of his will, and might get him to
declare it either by lightning or by the flight of
birds. And when men doubted whether Egeria
had really given him her counsel, she gave him a
sign by which he might prove it to them. He
called many of the Romans to supper, and set
before them a homely meal in earthen dishes; and
then on a sudden he said that now Egeria was
come to visit him. Straightway the dishes and
the cups became of gold or precious stones, and

the couches were covered with rare and costly coverings, and the meats and drinks were abundant and most delicious.

'Though Numa took so much care for the service of the gods, yet he forbade all costly sacrifices; neither did he suffer blood to be shed on the altars, nor any images of the gods to be made. But he taught the people to offer in sacrifice nothing but the fruits of the earth, meal, and cakes of flour, and roasted corn. For he loved husbandry, and he wished his people to live every man on his own inheritance in peace and in happiness. So the lands, which Romulus had won in war, he divided out amongst the people, and gave a certain portion to every man. He then ordered landmarks to be set on every portion; and Terminus the god of landmarks had them in his keeping, and he who moved a landmark was accursed. The craftsmen of the city, who had no land, were divided according to their callings; and there were made of them nine guilds. So all was peaceful and prosperous throughout the reign of Numa. The gates of the temple of Janus were never opened; for the Romans had no wars and no enemies. And Numa built a temple to Faith, and appointed a solemn worship for her, that men might learn not to lie or deceive, but to speak and act in honesty. And when he had lived to the age of fourscore years, he died at last by a gentle decay; and he was buried under the hill Janiculum

on the other side of the Tiber; and the books of
his sacred laws and ordinances were buried near
him in a separate tomb.'

It will be seen at a glance that a great part of
this narrative cannot be considered historical; it
is mythology pure and simple. Some Roman
writers attempted to frame a true history out of
the supernatural element in these early stories.
To take one example out of many,—wishing to
reduce the beautiful legend of the Translation of
Romulus to a probable history, they explained
the disappearance of the king by alleging that he
was torn limb from limb by the angry senators,
who carried away the pieces under their gowns.
Such a method is, of course, hopeless. We cannot
extract a true history out of materials which are
for the most part fabulous. We must content
ourselves with the belief that these legends merely
fill up the void left by a lost history. In
dealing with them, ' we are,' as has been well said,
' in a manner upon enchanted ground. Although
some real elements exist, yet the general picture
before us is a mere fantasy. Men love to complete
what is imperfect and to realise what is imaginary.'

By the side of the pure mythology in the
Numa legend we find another element,—that which
has to do with the origin of institutions. Pride
in their national customs was a leading feature
in the Roman character. The people loved to
have for them the sanction of divine authority.

Romulus, reputed to be the son of Mars, was naturally regarded as 'a man of war from his youth,'
with no time to spare for the establishment of
priesthoods, and ceremonies, and institutions. Accordingly, he is succeeded by a peaceful and saintly
monarch, who is represented as inaugurating at
once, under divine guidance, the complete religious
system which existed in later times, and other
institutions as well. Yet there is scarcely one of
the institutions ascribed to Numa which is not
attributed by other writers to some other king;
just as by the side of the story of the Twins and
the Foundation of Rome, which we find in Livy,
there existed about twenty rival narratives entirely
different from it. In view of such discrepancies,
we may well suppose that the institutions put
down to Numa grew up by slow degrees, and that
none of them can be traced to any particular
author.

It is important to observe that Livy himself
shows no signs of belief in Numa as a real person.
With all his genius for making the dead live again,
he does not attempt to clothe this shadowy saint
with flesh and blood. In fact, he is a thorough
sceptic about these early legends, and puts the
case against them with great force and frankness.
Looking back from the age of Augustus (i.e.
more than seven centuries after the beginning of
the era of the kings), he writes thus :—'The facts
of those early times are hardly visible through the

mists of antiquity. Written documents, the only safe shrine of history, were then meagre and few in number. The registers of the priests, together with other official and private records, almost all perished in the conflagration of the city.' Livy is referring to the burning of Rome by the Gauls in 390 B.C. The almost total destruction of documents and monuments of all kinds at this disastrous time is a fact of the first importance, when we are considering the trustworthiness of the story of the kings. The earliest historian of Rome was Quintus Fabius Pictor, whose work does not survive. He wrote more than 500 years after the foundation of the city; and he can have had at his disposal only a small number of documents and inscriptions, which had escaped the general havoc. Hence we may at once infer that the bulk of the history of the kings can have no better origin than transmission from mouth to mouth. Now, in Livy's record there are many scenes described with great minuteness. For example, the animated description of the combat between Horatii and Curiatii (ch. 9 of this book) is remarkable for its full details. It is impossible to believe that minute particulars like these could be passed on by oral tradition through several centuries. Such detailed descriptions must surely be due to the creative fancy of poet or novelist.

There are several striking examples of apparently pure fiction in the stories of the later kings,

—for instance, the lively description of Tanaquil's vigorous action after her husband's death (ch. 15). The stories of the stratagem by which Sextus Tarquinius took Gabii, and of the king and the poppies (ch. 18) have been attributed to a novelist familiar with Greek literature; for they appear to be directly copied from similar stories in the Greek historian Herodotus. Some have thought that all that is picturesque and poetical in the legends of the kings was due to a great series of ancient lays. Some such poems there doubtless were; but there is no evidence to show that they were many in number or that they played an important part in the making of the legends. 'Although,' writes Dr Arnold, 'verses were undoubtedly made and sung in the times of the kings, at funerals and at feasts, in commemoration of the worthy deeds of the noblest of the Romans; and although some of the actual stories of the kings may perhaps have come down from this source, yet it does not appear that they were ever written. Thus they were altered from one generation to another, nor can any one tell at what time they attained to their present shape. If this be so, there rests a veil not to be removed, not only on the history of the early Romans, but on that which we should much more desire to know, the nature and power of their genius,—what they thought, what they hated, and what they loved. Yet, although the legends of the early

Roman story are neither historical, nor yet coeval with the subjects which they celebrate, still their fame is so great and their beauty and interest so surpassing, that it would be unpardonable to sacrifice them altogether to the spirit of enquiry, and to exclude them from the place which they have so long held in Roman history.'

THE TRADITIONAL CHRONOLOGY OF THE
PERIOD OF THE KINGS.

ROME

IN EARLY TIMES.

a Temple of Jupiter.
c Comitium.
b Mouth of the Cloaca Maxima.
d Temple of Castor.
e Temple of Vesta.

THE STORY OF THE KINGS.

Birth and early years of Romulus and Remus.

1. Rea Silvia, Albāna sacerdōs, geminōs
puerōs ēdidit. Amūlius, rex crūdēlis, Silviam
in custōdiam dedit; puerōs in prōfluentem aquam
mittī iussit. forte eō tempore super rīpās Tiberis
effūsus erat. itaque in proximā ēluviē puerī sunt 5
expositī. paulisper alveus, in quō iacent, hūc
illūc fluitat. tandem tenuis aqua eōs in siccō
destituit. simul lupa sitiens ex montibus, quī
circā sunt, ad puerīlem vāgītum cursum flexit.
mox eam linguā lambentem puerōs Faustulus, 10
magister rēgiī pecoris, invēnit; quī Lārentiae
uxorī eōs ēducandōs dedit.

   ita genitī nūtrītīque sunt Rōmulus et Remus.
posteā, iam adultī, vēnandō saltūs peragrant.
hinc rōbur corporibus animīsque sūmunt. nec 15
iam ferās tantum agitant; sed in latrōnēs praedā
onustōs faciunt impetūs. pastōribus rapta dīvi-
dunt, et cum hīs sēria ac iocōs peragunt.

The new city.   The omens.   The slaying
of Remus.

2.   mox Rōmulus Remusque volēbant in iīs
locīs, ubi ēducāti erant, urbem condere.   hinc
foedum certāmen ā mītī principiō ortum est.
namque, quoniam geminī erant, aetās discrīmen
5 inter eōs facere nōn poterat.   'uter,' inquiunt,
'nōmen novae urbī dabit?   uter conditam imperiō
reget?'
      deōs igitur auguriō consulunt.   cūius causā
templa capiunt, Palātium Rōmulus, Remus Aven-
10 tīnum.   priorī Remō signum venit; cuī sex vulturēs
cito appārent.   hōc nuntiātō, duodecim Rōmulō
sēsē ostendunt.   utrumque rēgem suī comitēs
salūtāvērunt.   tempore enim illī, hī numerō avium
regnum sibi vindicābant.
15   inde cum magnīs clāmōribus congressī, ad
caedem vertuntur.   lūdibriō frātris Remus novōs
transiluit mūrōs.   statim ab īrātō Rōmulō ictus
cecidit.   tunc ille, 'sīc,' inquit, 'pereat, quīcumque alius transiliet moenia mea.'   ita sōlus potītus
20 est imperiō Rōmulus; condita urbs conditōris
nōmine appellāta est.

Mention of the worship of Hercules introduces
the story of Hercules and Cacus.

3.   Palātium prīmum, in quō ipse ēducātus
erat, Rōmulus mūnīvit.   sacra Graccō rītū Herculī

facit. Herculēs in ea loca, Gēryonē interemptō, bovēs mīrā speciē abēgerat. deinde prope Tiberim fluvium in locō herbidō, ut pābulō laetō reficeret 5 armentum, ipse, fessus viā, prōcubuit. ibi eum cibō vīnōque gravātum sopor oppressit.

pastor accola ēius locī, nōmine Cācus, ferox vīribus, boum pulchritūdine captus est. tantam praedam āvertendī cupidus, haec sēcum reputat: 10 'sī armentum in spēluncam meam compulerō, nonne ipsa vestīgia quaerentem dominum eō dē-dūcent?' itaque āversās bovēs, eximiā quamque formā, caudīs in spēluncam traxit.

prīmā lūce Herculēs somnō excitus est. cum 15 bovēs perlustrasset oculīs, partem abesse sensit. pergit ad proximam spēluncam, sī forte eō vestīgia ferrent. ubi ea omnia forās versa vīdit, incertus animī, agere porrō armentum coepit. deinde bovēs quaedam dēsīderiō relictārum, ut fit, mūgiē- 20 bant. statim reddita est vox boum ex spēlunca. cum Herculēs illūc properasset, Cācus eum vī prohibēre cōnātus est. sed ictus clāvā, auxilium pastōrum nēquīquam invocans, poenās dedit.

Growth of Rome. The Asylum. Seizure of the Sabine maidens. A trifling war.

4. urbs Rōma crescēbat mūnītiōnibus, cum in spē futūrae multitūdinis Rōmulus aedificāret. deinde novōs incolas allicere volēbat, nē vāna urbis magnitūdo esset. ita locum, quī nunc inter

5 duōs lūcōs saeptus est, asȳlum aperit. eō ex
fīnitimīs populīs magna turba, avida novārum
rērum, perfugit. vīrium rēgem haud paenitet.
tum consiliī cupidus, centum creat senātōrēs, quī
patrēs etiam dīcuntur; fīliīque eōrum patriciī
10 appellantur.

iam rēs Rōmāna maximē valēbat; sed manifesta erat pēnūria mulierum. Rōmulus igitur
lēgātōs circā vīcīnās gentēs mīsit, quī societātem
cōnūbiumque novō populō peterent. nusquam
15 autem benignē lēgātiō audīta est. adeō fīnitimī
simul Rōmam spernēbant, simul tantam mōlem in
mediō crescentem metuēbant. plērīque etiam rogi-
tant: 'num fēminīs quoque asȳlum aperuistis?'

aegrē id Rōmānī passī sunt; haud dubiē ad
20 vim spectāre rēs coepit. Rōmulus lūdōs sollemnēs
ex industriā parat. fīnitimī ad spectāculum hospitāliter invītantur. inter eōs Sabīnōrum omnis
multitūdo cum līberīs ac coniugibus vēnit. dum
lūdōs mīrantur, tum ex compositō vīs oritur;
25 signōque datō iuventūs Rōmāna ad rapiendās
virginēs discurrit. turbātō per metum lūdicrō,
Sabīnī parentēs prōfugiunt; incūsant hospitium
violātum, deōsque invocant. mox animī raptārum
mītigātī sunt; mātrimōniō contentae quiescēbant.
30 sed parentēs sordidā veste lacrimīsque et que-
rellīs congregābantur ad Titum Tātium, rēgem
Sabīnōrum. lentē agere hīs Tātius vīsus est.
itaque ipsī trēs populī, ad quōs ēius iniūriae pars
pertinēbat, commūniter bellum parant. effusē

vastantibus fit obvius cum exercitū Rōmulus; 35
levīque certāmine docet vānam sine vīribus īram
esse.

Another war. Tarpeia's treachery. Strange end-
    ing of a battle. Romans and Sabines form
    one state.

5. posteā Sabīnī acrius rem gerunt. iam
nihil per īram actum est; nec ostendērunt bellum
priusquam intulērunt. consiliō etiam additus
dolus. Spurius Tarpeius Rōmānae arcī praeerat.
hūius fīliam Tarpeiam Tātius novā quādam mer- 5
cēde corrumpit, ut armātōs in arcem accipiat.
vulgō Sabīnī aureās armillās bracchiō laevō gem-
mātōsque ānulōs habēbant. Tarpeia igitur, dē
pretiō prōditiōnis suae rogāta, respondit: 'date
mihi quod in sinistrīs manibus habētis.' itaque, in 10
arcem acceptī, perfidam virginem scūtīs obrutam
necāvēre.

tenuēre tamen arcem Sabīnī; atque posterō
diē acerrimē utrimque pugnātum est. sed rēs
Rōmāna erat superior. tum Sabīnae mulierēs, 15
quārum ex iniūriā bellum ortum erat, crīnibus
passīs inter tēla volantia sē inferre; impetū factō,
dirimere infestās aciēs; hīc patrēs, illīc virōs ōrāre,
nē sanguine nefandō socerī generīque sē respergerent. haec quoque clāmitant: 'sī cōnūbiī atque 20
adfīnitātis vōs piget, in nōs vertite īrās. nōs
causa vulnerum ac caedium virīs ac parentibus

sumus.   perīre mālumus quam viduae aut orbae
vīvere.'

25   movet rēs multitūdinem ac ducēs.   repentīna
fit quiēs; inde ad foedus faciendum ducēs prō-
deunt.   nec pācem modo, sed cīvitātem ūnam ex
duābus faciunt; regnum consociant; imperium
omne conferunt Rōmam.

The translation of Romulus.

6. immortālibus perfectīs operibus, forte Rōmulus exercitum recensēbat.   subitō coorta tempestās, cum magnō fragōre tonitrubusque, tam
densō rēgem operuit nimbō, ut conspectum ēius
5 populō abstulerit; nec deinde in terrīs Rōmulus
fuit.   mox serēna et tranquilla lux rediit.   Rōmāna
pūbēs, sēdātō tandem pavōre, vacuam sēdem rēgiam
vīdit.

satis crēdēbant patribus, quī proximī steterant,
10 sublīmem raptum esse procellā.   tamen, velut
orbitātis metū īctī, maestī diū silēbant.   deinde
deum deō nātum, rēgem parentemque urbis Rōmānae, salvēre Rōmulum iubent.   precibus ex-
poscunt ut propitius suam semper sospitet prō-
15 geniem.   fuisse crēdō aliquōs, quī discerptum
rēgem patrum manibus tacitī arguerent.   mānāvit
enim haec quoque fāma, sed perobscūra; illam
alteram admīrātiō virī et pavor praesens nōbili-
tāvit.

20   consiliō etiam ūnīus hominis reī fidēs additur.

namque Proculus Iūlius, sollicitā cīvitāte dēsīderiō
rēgis et infensa patribus, in contiōnem prōdit.
'Rōmulus,' inquit, 'Quirītēs, parens hūius urbis,
hodiē prīmā lūce, caelō repentē dēlapsus, sē mihi
obvium dedit. perfūsus horrōre, venerābundus 25
adstitī, petens precibus ut contrā intuēri fās esset.'
'abī, nuntiā,' inquit, 'Rōmānīs, caelestēs ita velle,
ut mea Rōma caput orbis terrārum sit. proinde
rem mīlitārem colant; sciantque et ita posterīs
trādant, nullās opēs hūmānās armīs Rōmānīs 30
resistere posse.' 'haec,' inquit, 'locūtus, sublīmis
abiit.' illī virō haec nuntiantī maximē crēditur.
dēsīderium Rōmulī apud plēbem exercitumque,
factā fidē immortālitātis, lēnītum est.

The reign of Numa, second king of Rome.

7. inclita iustitia religiōque eō tempore
Numae Pompiliī erat. Curibus Sabīnīs habitābat,
vir consultissimus omnis dīvīnī atque hūmānī iūris.
patrēs Rōmānī inclīnārī opēs ad Sabīnōs, rēge inde
sumptō, intellegunt. tamen, nēminem praeferre 5
illī virō ausī, ad ūnum omnēs Numae regnum
dēferendum dēcernunt.

ille accitus, sīcut Rōmulus auguriō regnum
adeptus est, dē sē quoque deōs consulī iussit.
inde ab augure dēductus in arcem, in lapide ad 10
merīdiem versus consēdit. augur ad laevam ēius,
capite vēlātō, sēdem cēpit, dextrā manū lituum
tenens. tum, lituō in laevam manum translātō,

dextrā in caput Numae impositā, precātus ita est:
15 'Iuppiter pater, sī est fās hunc Numam Pompilium,
cūius ego caput teneō, rēgem Rōmae esse, tū signa
certa dā nōbīs.' tum perēgit verbīs auspicia, quae
mittī vellet. quibus missīs, declārātus rex dē
templō descendit.

20   is, regnō ita potītus, urbem novam, conditam
vī et armīs, legibus ac mōribus dē integrō condere
parat. omnium prīmum multitūdinī iniciendum
deōrum metum ratus est; qui descendere ad animōs
sine aliquō commentō mīrāculī nōn poterat. ita
25 simulat sibi cum deā Ēgeriā congressūs nocturnōs
esse. ēius sē monitū, quae acceptissima dīs essent,
sacra instituere affirmat. īdem ad cursūs lūnae in
duodecim mensēs describit annum. omnium tamen
maximum ēius operum fuit tūtēla haud minor
30 pācis quam regnī. ita duo deinceps rēgēs, alius
aliā viā, ille bellō, hic pāce, cīvitātem auxērunt.
Rōmulus septem et trīgintā regnāvit annōs, Numa
trēs et quadrāgintā.

Tullus Hostilius, the third king. His
warlike character.

8.   post mortem Numae Tullum Hostīlium
rēgem esse populus iussit. hic nōn sōlum proximō
rēgī dissimilis, sed ferōcior etiam quam Rōmulus
fuit. senescere cīvitātem ōtiō ratus, causās bellī
5 undique quaerēbat. forte agrestēs Rōmānī ex
Albānō agrō, Albānī ex Rōmānō praedās agēbant.

hinc, Tullō auctōre, ortum est bellum. Albānī
priōrēs ingentī exercitū impetum faciunt; castra
ab urbe quinque millia passuum locant.
 in hīs castrīs Cluilius, Albānus rex, moritur. 10
dictātōrem Albānī Mettium Fūfetium creant. is
lēgātum praemīsit, quī Tullō nuntiāret opus esse
colloquiō, priusquam dīmicārent. cum paucīs
procerum in medium ducēs prōcēdunt. ibi infit
Albānus: 'cupīdō imperiī duōs cognātōs vīcīnōsque 15
populōs ad arma stimulat. nōn contentī lībertāte
certā, in dubiam imperiī servitiīque āleam īmus.
itaque, sī nōs dī amant, ineāmus aliquam viam,
quā hōc certāmen sine multō· sanguine dēcernī
possit.' haud displicet rēs Tullō. mox ratiō 20
initur, cuī et fortūna ipsa praebuit māteriam.

Combat between the Horatii and Curiatii.

9. forte in duōbus exercitibus erant trigeminī
frātrēs, nec aetāte nec vīribus disparēs. Horatiōs
Cūriātiōsque fuisse satis constat. tamen in rē
tam clārā nōminum error manet, utrīus populī
Horātiī, utrīus Cūriātiī fuerint. plūrēs tamen 5
inveniō auctōrēs quī Rōmānōs Horātiōs vocant.
hōs ut sequar inclīnat animus. priusquam dīmicārent, foedus ictum est inter Rōmānōs et Albānōs,
ut, cūius populī cīvēs vīcissent, is alterī populō
imperitāret.   10
 deinde trigeminī arma capiunt; ferōcēs in
medium inter duās aciēs prōcēdunt. consēderant

utrimque prō castrīs duo exercitūs; ērectī suspen-
sīque animō intenduntur.   datur signum, infestīs-
15 que armīs ternī iuvenēs, magnōrum exercituum
animōs gerentēs, concurrunt.   ut prīmō statim
concursū increpuēre arma, micantēsque fulsēre
gladiī, horror ingens spectantēs perstringit; torpē-
bat vox spīritusque.   duo Rōmānī, super alium
20 alius, vulnerātīs tribus Albānīs, exspīrantēs corru-
ērunt.   cum conclāmasset gaudiō Albānus exercitus, Rōmānās legiōnēs spēs tōta, nondum tamen
cūra, dēseruerat.

únum Rōmānum trēs Cūriātiī circumsteterant;
25 forte is integer fuit.   ergō, ut sēgregāret pugnam
eōrum, capessit fugam.   iam aliquantum spatiī
ex eō locō, ubi pugnātum est, aufūgerat, cum
respiciens videt magnīs intervallīs sequentes.   ūnus
haud procul aberat; in quem magnō impetū rediit.
30 et dum Albānus exercitus inclāmat Cūriātiīs, utī
opem ferant frātrī, iam Horātius, caesō hoste,
secundam pugnam petēbat.   tunc clāmōre Rōmānī
adiuvant mīlitem suum; et ille dēfungī praeliō
festīnat.   priusquam alter, quī nōn procul aberat,
35 consequī posset, alterum Cūriātium conficit.

itaque aequātō Marte singulī supererant, sed
nec spē nec vīribus parēs.   alter, intactus ferrō et
gemīnātā victōriā ferox, certāmen tertium inībat;
alter, fessum vulnere, fessum cursū trahens corpus,
40 victusque frātrum ante sē strāge, victōrī obicitur
hostī.   nec illud praelium fuit.   Rōmānus exultans
gladium in iugulō dēfīgit; iacentem spoliat.

amīcī ovantēs ac grātulantēs Horātium accipiunt, eō māiōre cum gaudiō, quō prope metum rēs fuerat. ad sepulturam inde suōrum, nēquāquam 45 paribus animīs, vertuntur, imperiō alterī auctī, alterī diciōnī aliēnae subiectī.

Horatius slays his sister. His trial.

10. Horātius ībat trigemina spolia prae sē gerens. cuī soror virgō, quae desponsa ūnī ex Cūriātiīs fuerat, obvia ante portam Capēnam fuit. cognitōque super humerōs frātris palūdāmentō sponsī, quod ipsa confēcerat, solvit crīnēs et 5 flēbiliter nōmine sponsum mortuum appellat. movet ferōcis iuvenis animum complōrātiō sorōris in victōriā suā tantōque gaudiō pūblicō. itaque strictō gladiō, simul verbīs increpans, transfīgit puellam. 'abī hinc cum immātūrō amōre ad 10 sponsum,' inquit, 'oblīta frātrum mortuōrum vīvīque, oblīta patriae. sīc eat quaecumque Rōmāna lūgēbit hostem.'

atrox vīsum id facinus patribus plēbīque; sed recens meritum factō obstābat. tamen raptus est 15 in iūs ad rēgem. tum Horātius, auctōre Tullō, clemente lēgis interprete, 'prōvocō,' inquit. ita de prōvocātiōne certātum est ad populum. Pūblius Horātius pater prōclāmāvit sē fīliam iūre caesam iūdicāre. ōrābat deinde nē sē, quem cum ēgregiā 20 stirpe conspexissent, orbum līberīs facerent. inter haec senex iuvenem amplexus, 'huncine,' āiēbat,

'quem modo ovantem vīdistis, sub furcā vinctum
inter verbera et cruciātūs vidēre potestis?' ī, lictor,
25 colligā manūs, quae paulō ante armātae imperium
populō Rōmānō peperērunt. ī, caput obnūbe
līberātōris urbis hūius; arbore infēlīcī suspende;
verberā, modo inter illa spolia hostium, modo inter
sepulcra Cūriātiōrum.' nōn tulit populus nec
30 patris lacrimās nec ipsīus parem in omnī perīculō
animum; absolvitque eum magis admīrātiōne
virtūtis quam iūre causae.

War with Fidenae and Veii. The treachery of
Mettius and its punishment. Tullus removes
the Albans to Rome.

11. nec diū pax Albāna mansit. invidia
vulgī, quod tribus mīlitibus fortūna pūblica com-
missa fuerit, Mettium corrūpit. quī ad bellum
palam aliōs concitat populōs, suīs per speciem
5 sociētātis prōditiōnem reservat. Fīdēnātēs, colōnia
Rōmāna, Veientibus sociīs adsumptīs, ad arma
incitantur. cum Fīdēnae apertē descissent, Tullus,
Mettiō exercitūque ēius ab Albā accītō, contrā
hostēs profectus est. fūsō Fīdēnātium cornū, in
10 Veientēs ferōcior redit. nec illī tulēre impetum;
sed ab effūsā fugā flūmen obiectum ab tergō
arcēbat. quō postquam fuga inclīnāvit, aliī, arma
foedē iactantēs, in aquam caecī ruēbant; aliī, dum
cunctantur in rīpīs, inter fugae pugnaeque con-

silium oppressī. nōn alia ante Rōmāna pugna 15
atrōcior fuit.

in hōc certāmine rēgī Rōmānō manifesta fuit
Mettī perfidia. is Tullō dēvictōs hostēs grātulātur;
contrā Tullus Mettium benignē alloquitur. cen-
turiōnēs tamen Rōmānī eum armātī circumsistunt. 20
rex sīc Albānīs orsus est : 'quod fēlix faustumque
sit—populum omnem Albānum Rōmam trādūcere
in animō est, ūnam urbem, ūnam rem pūblicam
facere.' ad haec Albāna pūbēs, inermis ab armātīs
saepta, commūnī metū cōgente, silentium tenet. 25
tum Tullus, 'Mettī Fūfetī,' inquit, 'quoniam tuum
insānābile ingenium est, at tū tuō suppliciō docē
hūmānum genus ea sancta crēdere, quae a tē
violāta sunt. ut igitur paulō ante animum inter
Fīdēnātēs Rōmānōsque ancipitem gessistī, ita iam 30
corpus passim distrahendum dabis.' exinde duābus
admōtīs quadrīgīs, in currūs eārum illigat Mettium.
deinde in dīversum iter equī concitātī lacerum
prōditōris corpus distraxēre.

inter haec iam praemissī Albam erant equitēs, 35
quī multitūdinem trādūcerent Rōmam. legiōnēs
deinde ductae ad dīruendam urbem. ēgressīs
Albānīs, Rōmānī omnia tecta adaequant solō ;
ūnāque hōrā quadringentōrum annōrum opus, per
quōs Alba steterat, excidiō ac ruīnīs dedēre. 40
templīs tamen deum—ita enim ēdictum ā rēge
erat—temperātum est. Rōma interim crescit
Albae ruīnīs. duplicātur cīvium numerus; Caelius
mons additur urbī. principēs Albānōrum Tullus
in senātum legit. 45

*Ancus Marcius, the fourth king. Additions to
the city. The coming of the Tarquins.*

12. Tullus magnā glōriā bellī regnāvit annōs
duōs et trīgintā. quō mortuō, Ancum Marcium,
Numae nepōtem, rēgem populus creāvit ; patrēs
fuēre auctōrēs. cīvibus ōtiī cupidīs et fīnitimīs
5 cīvitātibus facta spēs novum rēgem avī in institūta
abitūrum. igitur Latīnī, cum quibus, Tullō
regnante, ictum foedus erat, sustulerant animōs.
cum incursiōnem in agrum Rōmānum fēcissent,
repetentibus rēs Rōmānīs superbē responsum red-
10 dunt ; namque dēsidem Rōmānum rēgem inter
sacella et ārās actūrum esse regnum ratī sunt.
Ancus tamen, exercitū novō conscriptō, urbēs
quasdam Latīnōrum vī cēpit.

secūtus mōrem rēgum priōrum, quī rem Rō-
15 mānam auxerant hostibus in cīvitātem accipiendīs,
multitūdinem omnem Rōmam trāduxit. et cum
circā Palātium, sēdem veterem Rōmānōrum, Sabīnī
Capitōlium atque arcem, Caelium montem Albānī
implessent, Aventīnum novae multitūdinī datum.
20 Iāniculum quoque adiectum. id nōn mūrō sōlum,
sed etiam ponte Subliciō, tum prīmum in Tiberī
factō, coniungī urbī placuit. Quirītium quoque
fossa, haud parvum mūnīmentum, Ancī rēgis opus
est. carcer ad terrōrem crescentis audāciae mediā
25 urbe, imminens forō, aedificātur. nec urbs tantum
hōc rēge crēvit, sed etiam ager fīnēsque. silva
Mēsia Veientibus adempta ; usque ad mare im-

perium prōlātum; et in ōre Tiberis Ostia urbs
condita; salīnae circā factae.

Ancō regnante, Lucumō, vir impiger ac dīvitiīs 30
potens, Rōmam migrāvit spē magnī honōris; cūius
adipiscendī Tarquiniīs—nam ibi quoque peregrīnus
erat—facultās nōn fuerat. ducta etiam in mātrimōnium Tanaquil, summō locō nāta, spernentibus
Etruscīs Lucumōnem, ferre indignitātem nōn 35
potuit. oblīta ingenitae ergā patriam cāritātis,
dummodo virum honōrātum vidēret, consilium
migrandī ā Tarquiniīs cēpit. Rōma ad id potis-
sima vīsa est. in novō populō, ubi omnis repentīna
nōbilitās esset, spērābant futūrum locum fortī ac 40
strēnuō virō.

sublātīs itaque rēbus, migrant Rōmam. ad
Iāniculum forte ventum erat; ibi eī, carpentō
sedentī cum uxōre, aquila demissa pilleum aufert,
superque carpentum cum magnō clangōre volitans 45
rursus capitī aptē repōnit; inde sublīmis abit.
accēpisse id augurium laeta dīcitur Tanaquil,
perīta, ut vulgō Etruscī, caelestium prōdigiōrum
mulier. excelsa et alta spērāre complexa virum
iubet. hās spēs sēcum portantēs, urbem ingressī 50
sunt. Lucumō L. Tarquinius Priscus appellātus
est. mox in rēgiam de eō fāma perlāta est. in
amīcitiam ā rēge acceptus, pūblicīs pariter ac
prīvātīs consiliīs mīlitiae domīque intererat. in
omnibus rēbus spectātus, postrēmō tūtor etiam 55
līberīs rēgis testāmentō institūtus est.

Tarquinius Priscus, the fifth king. His wars.
The razor and the whetstone.

13. regnāvit Ancus annōs quattuor et vīgintī,
cuīlibet superiōrum rēgum bellī pācisque artibus
et gloriā pār. iam fīliī ēius adolescēbant. eō
magis Tarquinius instāre, ut quam prīmum comitia
5 rēgī creandō fierent. quibus indictīs, sub tempus
puerōs vēnātum mīsit. isque prīmus et petiisse
ambitiōsē regnum et ōrātiōnem dicitur habuisse ad
conciliandōs plēbis animōs compositam. ingentī
consensū populus Rōmānus eum regnāre iussit.
10 ille bellum prīmum cum Latīnīs gessit; prae-
dāque inde maximā revectā, lūdōs opulentius quam
priōrēs rēgēs fēcit. tunc prīmum circō, quī nunc
maximus dīcitur, dēsignātus locus est. mūrō
quoque lapideō circumdare urbem parābat, cum
15 Sabīnum bellum coeptīs intervēnit. adeōque ea
subita rēs fuit, ut Aniēnem transīrent hostēs,
priusquam prohibēre exercitus Rōmānus posset.
itaque trepidātum Rōmae est. et primō dubia
victōria, magnā utrimque caede pugnātum est.
20 reductīs deinde in castra hostium cōpiīs, datur
spatium Rōmānīs ad parandum dē integrō bellum.

Tarquinius, equitem maximē suīs dēesse vīribus
ratus, centuriās equitum vult constituere. negat
Attius Navius, inclitus eō tempore augur, hōc fierī
25 posse, nisi avēs coeptō fāvissent. īrātus rex, 'age,'
inquit, 'dīvīne tū, dic, fierīne possit quod nunc
ego mente concipiō.' cum ille auguriō rem

expertus futūram dixisset, 'atquī hōc animō
agitāvī,' inquit, 'tē novāculā cōtem discissūrum.
cape haec, et perage quod avēs tuae fierī posse 30
portendunt.' tum illum haud cunctanter discidisse
cōtem ferunt. statua Attī capite vēlātō, quō in
locō rēs acta est, in comitiō fuit. cōtem quoque
eōdem locō sitam fuisse memorant, ut esset
mīrāculī ēius monumentum. auguriīs certē tantus 35
honor accessit, ut nihil bellī domīque posteā, nisi
auspicātō, gererētur, concilia populī exercitūsque
vocātī, ubi avēs nōn admīsissent, dirimerentur.

mox iterum cum Sabīnīs conflīgitur. iam vīribus
crēverat Rōmānus exercitus; ex occultō etiam 40
additur dolus. missī sunt quī magnam vim
lignōrum, in rīpā Aniēnis iacentem, in flūmen
ardentem cōnicerent. ventōque iuvante, accensa
ligna, cum sublicīs haerērent, pontem incendunt.
ea quoque rēs in pugnā terrōrem tulit Sabīnīs, 45
et fugam impediit; multique mortālēs, cum hostem
effūgissent, in flūmine ipsō periēre. quōrum arma
fluitantia ad urbem, vīsa in Tiberī, priusquam
nuntiārī posset, insignem victōriam fēcēre. bellō
Sabīnō perfectō, Tarquinius triumphans Rōmam 50
redit. inde Latīnīs bellum fēcit. ad singula
oppida circumferendō arma, omne nōmen Latīnum
domuit. pax deinde est facta.

Servius Tullius. The miracle of his childhood.

14. eō tempore in regiā prōdigium vīsum,
ēventūque mīrābile fuit. puerō dormientī, cuī

Serviō Tulliō fuit nōmen, caput arsisse ferunt
multōrum in conspectū. plūrimō igitur clāmōre
5 ortō, cum quīdam familiārium aquam ad restin-
guendum ferret, ā rēgīnā retentus est; quae, sēdātō
tumultū, movērī vetuit puerum, dōnec suā sponte
experrectus esset. mox cum somnō flamma quoque
abiit. tum, abductō in secretum virō, Tanaquil,
10 'viden tu puerum hunc,' inquit, 'quem tam humilī
cultū educāmus? scīre licet hunc lūmen quondam
rēbus nostrīs dubiīs futūrum praesidiumque rēgiae
afflictae. proinde māteriam ingentis decoris omnī
indulgentiā nostrā nūtriāmus.' inde puer in
15 cāritāte atque honōre erat. ēvenit facile quod
diīs cordī est; iuvenis ēvāsit vērē indolis rēgiae;
et, cum quaererētur gener Tarquiniō, fīliam ēī
suam rex despondit. tantus illī honōs habitus
crēdere prohibet servā nātum eum parvumque
20 ipsum servisse.

Murder of Tarquinius Priscus. Tanaquil's
presence of mind.

15. duodēquadrāgēsimō fermē annō, ex quō
regnāre coeperat Tarquinius, nōn apud rēgem
modo, sed apud patrēs plēbemque, maximō honōre
Servius Tullius erat. tum Ancī fīliī duo putābant
5 praecipuē id domūs suae rēgiae dēdecus fore, sī
nōn modo advenīs, sed servīs etiam regnum patēret.
Servium enim servā nātum esse affirmābant. ferrō
igitur eam arcēre contumēliam statuunt; ipsī rēgī

insidiās parant. ex pastōribus duo ferōcissimī
dēlectī ad facinus. in vestibulō rēgiae tumultuō- 10
sissimē, speciē rixae, in sē omnēs apparitōrēs rēgis
convertunt. inde, cum ambō rēgem appellārent,
vocātī ad ipsum pergunt. prīmō vōciferārī et
certātim alter alterī obstrepere. coercitī a lictōre
et iussī invicem dīcere, tandem obloquī dēsistunt. 15
ūnus rem ex compositō ordītur. dum intentus in
eum sē rex āvertit, alter clātam secūrim in caput
dēiēcit, relictōque in vulnere tēlō, ambō sē forās
ēiciunt.

Tarquinium moribundum cum quī circā erant 20
excēpissent, illōs fugientēs lictōrēs comprehendunt.
clāmor inde concursusque mīrantium. Tanaquil
inter tumultum claudī rēgiam iubet. Serviō
properē accītō cum paene exsanguem virum
ostendisset, dextram tenens ōrat, ne inultam esse 25
mortem socerī sinat. 'tuum est,' inquit, 'Servī,
sī vir es, regnum, nōn eōrum quī aliēnīs manibus
pessimum facinus fēcēre. ērige tē deōsque ducēs
sequere, quī clārum hōc fore caput, dīvīnō quondam
circumfūsō ignī, portendērunt. nunc tē illa 30
caelestis excitet flamma; nunc expergiscere vērē.
et nōs peregrīnī regnāvimus. quī sīs, nōn unde
nātus sīs, reputā. si tua rē subitā consilia torpent,
at tū mea sequere.'

cum clāmor impetusque multitūdinis vix 35
sustinerī posset, ex superiōre parte aedium per
fenestrās populum Tanaquil alloquitur. iubet
bonō animō esse; sōpītum fuisse rēgem affirmat

subitō ictū; ferrum haud altē in corpus descendisse;
40 iam ad sē eum redisse; inspectum vulnus, abstersō
cruōre; omnia salūbria esse; mox ipsum eōs
vīsūrōs; interim Servium Tullium iūra redditūrum,
obitūrumque alia rēgis mūnia esse.

Servius Tullius, the sixth king. His work.

16. Servius cum trabeā et lictōribus prōdit;
ac sēde rēgiā sedens alia dēcernit, dē aliīs sē rēgem
consultūrum esse simulat. itaque per aliquot diēs,
cum iam exspīrasset Tarquinius, cēlātā morte suās
5 opēs firmāvit. tum dēmum palam factum est
complōrātiōne in rēgiā ortā. Servius praesidiō
firmō mūnītus regnāvit. Ancī līberī, iam com-
prensīs sceleris ministrīs, ut tantās esse opēs Serviī
nuntiātum est, in exilium ierant.
10 opportūnē bellum cum Veientibus aliīsque
Etruscīs sumptum. in eō bellō et virtūs et
fortūna ēnituit Tulliī; fūsōque ingentī hostium
exercitū, haud dubius rex Rōmam rediit. ag-
grediturque inde ad pācis longē maximum opus,
15 ut Servium auctōrem omnium in cīvitāte ordinum
graduumque dignitātis posterī fāmā ferant. censum enim instituit, rem salūberrimam tantō futūrō
imperiō, ex quō bellī pacisque mūnia prō opibus
cūiusque fierent. tum classēs centuriāsque ex
20 censū descripsit.

urbs quoque amplificanda vīsa est; addit duōs
collēs, Quirīnālem Vīminālemque; inde deinceps

Rōmam auget Esquiliīs, ibique ipse, ut locō
dignitās fieret, habitat. aggere et fossīs et mūrō
circumdat urbem. regnāvit annōs quattuor et 25
quadrāgintā, ita ut bonō etiam moderātōque
succēdentī rēgi difficilis aemulātiō esset. id quoque ad glōriam accessit, quod cum illō simul iusta
ac lēgitima regna occidērunt. id ipsum tam mīte
ac tam moderātum imperium tamen dēpōnere in 30
animō habuisse dīcitur; sed scelus domesticum
līberandae patriae consilia agitantī intervēnit.

Tarquinius Superbus, the seventh and last
king. His tyranny.

17. crēditur, quia nōn abhorret ā cētero
scelere, Tulliae, iussū Servium esse interfectum.
carpentō certē in forum invecta ēvocāvit virum ē
cūriā, rēgemque prīma appellāvit. cum ea sē
domum reciperet, restitit pavidus atque inhibuit 5
frēnōs is quī equōs agēbat, iacentemque dominae
Servium trucīdātum ostendit. foedum inhūmān-
umque inde trāditur scelus, monumentōque locus
est. Scelerātum vīcum vocant, quō āmens furiīs
Tullia per patris corpus carpentum ēgisse fertur, 10
partemque sanguinis paternī tulisse ad penātēs
suōs.

inde L. Tarquinius regnāre coepit, cuī Superbō
cognōmen facta dedērunt, quia socerum sepultūrā
prohibuit, Rōmulum quoque insepultum periisse 15
dictitans; prīmōrēsque patrum, quōs Servii rēbus

fāvisse crēdēbat, interfēcit.　hic rēgum prīmus
trāditum ā priōribus mōrem dē omnibus senātum
consulendī solvit; domesticīs consiliīs rem pūblicam
20 administrāvit; bellum, pācem, foedera, societātēs
per sē ipse, cum quibus voluit, iniussū populī ac
senātūs, fēcit dirēmitque.

ad negōtia urbāna animum convertit; quōrum
erat prīmum, ut Iovis templum, monumentum
25 regnī suī nōminisque, relinqueret.　secūtum est
magnitūdinem imperiī portendens prōdigium:
caput hūmānum integrā faciē aperientibus funda-
menta templī dīcitur appāruisse; quae vīsa speciēs
haud per ambāgēs arcem eam imperiī caputque
30 rērum fore portendēbat.　intentus perficiendō
templō, fabrīs undique ex Etrūriā accītīs, nōn
pecūnia sōlum ad id pūblicā est ūsus, sed operīs
etiam ex plēbe.　quī cum haud parvus mīlitiae
adderētur labor, minus tamen plebs nōlēbat templa
35 deum aedificāre manibus suīs.

Gabii is taken by treachery.　The king and the poppy-heads.

18.　rex Gabiōs, propinquam urbem, nēquīquam vī adortus, postrēmō minimē arte Rōmānā,
fraude ac dolō, aggressus est.　Sextus fīlius ēius
transfūgit ex compositō Gabiōs, patris in sē
5 saevitiam intolerābilem conquerens.　benignē ā
Gabīnīs excipitur.　cum sensim ad rebellandum
prīmōrēs cīvitātis incitāret, ipse cum promptissimīs

iuvenum praedātum īret, dux ad ultimum bellī
legitur. ibi cum praelia parva inter Rōmam
Gabiōsque fierent, plērumque Gabīna rēs superior 10
erat. tum certātim summī infimīque Gabīnōrum
Sextum Tarquinium dōnō deōrum sibi missum
ducem crēdere.

itaque postquam satis vīrium collectum ad
omnēs cōnātūs vidēbat, tum ex suīs ūnum Rōmam 15
ad patrem mittit, sciscitātum quidnam sē facere
vellet. huīc nuntiō, quia, crēdō, dubiae fideī
vidēbātur, nihil vōce responsum est. rex, velut
dēlīberābundus, in hortum aedium transit, sequente
nuntiō fīliī; ibi inambulans tacitus summa papā- 20
verum capita dīcitur baculō dēcussisse. inter-
rogandō exspectandōque responsum nuntius fessus,
ut rē imperfectā, redit Gabiōs. quae dixerit ipse
quaeque vīderit, refert; seu īrā seu odiō seu superbiā insitā nullam eum vōcem emīsisse. Sextus, 25
ubi quid parens praeciperet tacitīs ambāgibus
intellexit, prīmōrēs Gabīnōrum multōs palam,
aliōs clam interfēcit. patuit quibusdam volentibus
fuga, aut in exilium actī sunt. absentium bona
atque interemptōrum populō dīvīsa sunt. ita 30
dulcēdine prīvātī commodī sensus malōrum pūbli-
cōrum adimī, dōnec, orba consiliō auxiliōque,
Gabīna rēs rēgī Rōmānō sine ullā dīmicātiōne in
manum trāditur.

A mission to Delphi. Brutus proves no dullard.

19. hōc ferē tempore portentum terribile
vīsum; anguis ex columnā ligneā ēlapsus, cum
terrōrem in rēgiā fēcisset, ipsīus rēgis pectus anxiīs
implēvit cūrīs. itaque cum ad pūblica prōdigia
5 Etruscī tantum vātēs adhibērentur, hōc velut
domesticō exterritus vīsū, Delphōs ad maximē
inclitum in terrīs ōrāculum mittere statuit. neque
responsa ullī aliī committere ausus, duōs fīliōs per
ignōtās eo tempore terrās, ignōtiōra maria, in
10 Graeciam mīsit. Titus et Arruns profectī. comes
iīs additus L. Iūnius Brūtus, Tarquiniā sorōre
rēgis nātus, iuvenis longē alius ingeniō, quam cūius
simulātiōnem induerat. ex industriā factus ad
imitātiōnem stultitiae, cum sē suaque praedae esse
15 rēgī sineret, Brūtī quoque haud abnuit cognōmen.
sub ēius obtentū cognōminis līberātor ille populī
Rōmānī animus latens opperiēbātur tempora sua.

is tum a Tarquiniīs ductus est Delphōs,
lūdibrium vērius quam comes. quō postquam
20 ventum est, perfectīs patris mandātīs, iuvenēs
sciscitantur, ad quem ex sē regnum Rōmānum
esset venturum. ex infimō specū vōcem redditam
ferunt: 'imperium summum Rōmae habēbit quī
vestrum prīmus, iuvenēs, osculum mātrī tulerit.'
25 Tarquinii inter sē, uter prior, cum Rōmam redis-
sent, mātrī osculum dāret, sortī permittunt.
Brūtus, aliō ratus spectāre Pȳthicam vōcem, velut

sī prōlapsus cecidisset, terram osculō contigit,
scīlicet quod ea commūnis māter omnium mortā-
lium esset. reditum inde Rōmam.   30

Expulsion of the Tarquins. The first consuls.

20. tandem Rōmānōs taedet domīnātiōnis
iniustae Tarquiniōrum. ā Brūtō ōrātiō habita
est nēquāquam ēius ingeniī, quod simulātum ad
eam diem fuerat, dē vī ac superbiā rēgis, miseriīs-
que et labōribus plēbis in fossās cloācāsque dē- 5
mersae; Rōmānōs hominēs, victōrēs omnium circā
populōrum, opificēs ac lapicīdās prō bellātōribus
factōs. hīs atrōciōribusque aliīs incensam multitūdinem perpulit, ut imperium rēgī abrogāret,
exulēsque esse iubēret L. Tarquinium cum coniuge 10
ac līberīs. ipse, iūniōribus, quī ultrō nōmina
dabant, lectīs armātīsque, Ardeam in castra est
profectus.

hārum rērum nuntiīs in castra perlātīs, cum rē
novā trepidus rex pergeret Rōmam ad compri- 15
mendōs mōtūs, flexit viam Brūtus, nē obvius fieret;
eōdemque ferē tempore dīversīs itineribus Brūtus
Ardeam, Tarquinius Rōmam vēnērunt. Tarquiniō
clausae portae exiliumque indictum. līberātōrem
urbis laeta castra accēpēre, exactīque inde līberī 20
rēgis. duo patrem secūtī sunt, quī exulātum in
Etruscōs iērunt. Sextus Tarquinius Gabiōs, tam-
quam in suum regnum, profectus, ab ultōribus

veterum simultātium est interfectus. L. Tarquinius
25 Superbus regnāvit annōs quinque et vīgintī.
regnātum Rōmae ab conditā urbe ad līberātam
annōs ducentōs quadrāgintā quattuor. duo con-
sulēs inde creātī sunt, L. Iūnius Brūtus et L. Tarquinius Collātīnus.

NOTES.

CHAPTER 1.

1. Albana, 'belonging to Alba.' The full name of the city
was Alba Longa, 'the Long White City.' It was long and
narrow, owing to the steepness of the mountain-side on which
it was built. Alba was the head of the league of Latin towns,
till Rome conquered her own mother-city and took her place.
The exact site of Alba is unknown.

geminos pueros. Mars was the father of the Twins,
according to the legend.

6. iacent—fluitat, historic presents, used to call up a
vivid picture, **337.** Compare several instances in the next
paragraph.

10. lingua lambentem pueros. Hence in Macaulay's
Horatius the Romans are called 'the she-wolf's litter.'

12. educandos dedit. See **384.**

14. venando, ablative of manner, **378.**

15. corporibus animisque, datives of advantage.

17. pastoribus, 'among the shepherds,' dative similar to
that after verbs of *giving*.

CHAPTER 2.

6. **conditam**, ' the city when it has been built,' 391.

8. **augurio**, ablative of manner.

9. **templa**, ' circuits,' ' districts.' The literal meaning of *templum* is a ' space marked off,' *i.e.* by the augur's staff, for the purpose of taking omens. Hence it means ' sacred enclosure,' and then ' temple.'

Palatium—Aventinum, ' the Palatine—the Aventine,' two of the seven hills on which Rome stood, when complete. See Plan of Rome.

11. **hoc nuntiato**. See 237.

12. **utrumque—salutaverunt**, ' each of them was hailed as king by his comrades.' If we translate thus, we can see why *sui* is used.

13. **tempore**, ' by priority in time,' ablative of cause.

illi, the supporters of Remus ; **hi**, of Romulus.

16. **ludibrio**, ' in mockery,' ablative of manner.

fratris, objective genitive, 262 (*a*).

18. **pereat**, subjunctive expressing a wish, 359.

20. **imperio**. See 242.

conditoris nomine. Livy's etymology is at fault. *Roma* cannot be derived from *Romulus*. It probably means ' River-town,' its situation in this respect being unique among the early towns of Latium. Some were clustered on and round the Alban hills; others lined the sea-coast.

CHAPTER 3.

1. **Palatium primum**. The first Roman settlement on the Palatine was sometimes called *Roma quadrata*, ' square Rome,' from the quadrilateral shape of the hill.

3. **Geryone interempto**. Geryon, a monster with three bodies and powerful wings, lived in Erytheia, a fabulous island in the western Mediterranean. The slaying of Geryon and the capture of his famous oxen formed one of the twelve labours of Hercules, who, on his return, passed through Gaul and Italy.

4. **mira specie**, ablative of quality, 234.

8. **ferox viribus,** 'proud of his strength.' Note that *ferox* generally means 'high-spirited,' 'warlike,' or 'proud,' not 'ferocious' or 'savage.' For the construction see **241.**

10. **avertendi cupidus, 376.** *avertere* is the regular word for 'lifting' cattle.

11. **compulero—deducent.** For this form of conditional sentence see **438.**

13. **eximia forma.** Compare l. 4 *mira specie.*

quamque, 'each,' in apposition to *boves.*

17. **si forte—ferrent,** '(to see) if perchance the footmarks led thither.'

19. **animi,** 'in mind,' not genitive, but old locative case. Compare *domi* 'at home,' *humi* 'on the ground.' See **246** (note).

20. **ut fit,** 'as usually happens,' *i.e.* 'naturally.'

CHAPTER **4.**

3. **ne—esset,** final clause, **423.**

4. **nunc,** *i.e.* in the time of the Emperor Augustus, when Livy wrote his history.

5. **asylum,** 'as an asylum.' *asylum* is a word borrowed from the Greek, meaning 'sanctuary' or 'place of refuge.' The place mentioned is between the Capitol and the Citadel; see Plan.

6. **avida novarum rerum,** 'eager for a new life.'

7. **virium regem haud paenitet.** For the construction see **288.** 'The king was well satisfied with the power he had gained. Next, anxious to have a body of advisers (*consilium*), he appointed a hundred senators.'

9. **patricii,** 'men of the Fathers,' 'Fathers' sons' (because they alone, in the eyes of the law, had a father), as opposed to 'plebeians' (the men of the commons).

13. **qui—peterent,** final clause, **423** (note 3).

14. **novo populo,** dative of advantage.

15. **adeo—metuebant.** In English we should make the first clause subordinate:—'To such an extent did her neigh-

bours, while they affected to despise Rome, all the time dread the growing power which loomed so large in their midst.'

21. **ex industria,** 'on purpose.' For the idiomatic use of *ex* cf. l. 24 *ex composito*, and see **286.**

22. **Sabinorum.** For the Sabine country see Map.

25. **ad rapiendas virgines,** another method of expressing purpose, frequently employed by Livy.

27. **incusant hospitium violatum,** 'they lay to their charge the violation of hospitality.' This participial construction is illustrated in **393.**

29. **matrimonio.** See **243.**

30. **sordida veste,** 'shabby clothes,' our 'mourning,' afterwards regularly assumed by defendants in the Roman law-courts to attract pity.

35. **vastantibus,** dative with *fit obvius,*—'meets them while they are ravaging (Roman territory) in disorder.'

CHAPTER 5.

2. **per iram,** 'in an ill-tempered way.' *per* often denotes manner, **285.**

nec ostenderunt—intulerunt, 'and they made no parade of war till they actually brought it upon Rome,' *i.e.* they kept their plan of campaign a secret.

3. **consilio—dolus,** 'treachery also was called in to the aid of policy.'

additus, for *additus est*, a frequent omission.

11. **obrutam necavere,** 'killed her by overwhelming her.'

13. **tamen,** 'however,' *i.e.* though they had gained it by foul means.

14. **pugnatum est.** See **301.**

17. **inferre—dirimere—orare,** historic infinitives, **372.**

18. **hic,** on the Sabine side; **illic,** on the Roman.

19. **ne—respergerent,** 'not to sprinkle themselves with impious blood, fathers-in-law and sons-in-law as they were.'

20. **conubii—vos piget.** See **288.**

26. **ad foedus faciendum.** Compare c. 4, l. 25.

28. **imperium—Romam,** 'concentrate all the sovereignty in Rome.'

CHAPTER **6**.

4. **ut—abstulerit.** For this sequence after the historic perfect see **422** (note 2).

5. **populo,** dative, **220**.

12. **deo,** ablative of origin.

13. **salvere Romulum iubent,** 'bid Romulus be well,' *i.e.* 'bid him all hail.'

16. **arguerent,** subjunctive due to *oratio obliqua.*

23. **Quirites** probably meant 'spearmen' originally.

26. **ut—esset,** 'that he might be suffered to gaze on him face to face.'

29. **colant—sciant—tradant.** Compare c. 2, l. 18.

32. **illi viro—creditur.** For the impersonal construction see **302**.

34. **facta fide immortalitatis,** 'when belief in his immortality was established.'

CHAPTER **7**.

2. **Curibus Sabinis,** 'at Cures in the Sabine territory.' See Map.

3. **consultissimus—iuris.** See **262** (*b*).

4. **inclinari—intellegunt.** Mark the force of the tense of *inclinari,*—'The Roman elders see that power is *there and then* shifting to the Sabines, if a king is chosen from that people.'

6. **ad unum,** 'to a man,' 'unanimously.'

10. **deductus,** 'conducted solemnly.' The word may be used of leading up as well as down.

arcem. The Citadel is marked in the Plan.

lapide, the Augural Stone.

16. **regem Romae,** not 'king *of* Rome,' which would be *regem Romanum,* but 'king *at* Rome,' *Romae* being the old locative case, **272** (*a*).

18. **vellet,** subjunctive because it is in virtual *oratio obliqua,* **469**.

declaratus, 'manifested' to be king by the signs, not 'declared' so by the augur.

19. **de templo**⎫
21. **de integro**⎭ . See **286**.

25. **Egeria.** See Introduction, p. viii.

27. **idem** should be here translated 'he also.'

CHAPTER **8**.

2. **populus iussit**, by a vote in their assembly. The approval (*auctoritas*) of the Senate was also necessary; see c. 12, l. 3.

3. **ferocior.** See c. 3, l. 8.

7. **Tullo auctore**, 'through the influence of Tullus,' **237**.

9. **quinque millia passuum**, 'at a distance of five miles,' **282**. *mille passuum* is 1000 Roman 'paces' (or double-steps) of five feet. Our military pace (= Roman *gradus*) is 2½ feet.

12. **opus esse colloquio.** See **243**.

17. **in dubiam—aleam imus**, 'we are courting the doubtful hazard of empire or slavery.' *alea* means originally 'a game at dice.'

18. **si nos di amant**, 'by the favour of heaven.'

19. **qua—possit**, final clause. Compare c. 4, l. 13.

21. **cui—materiam**, 'for which also Fortune herself provided the opportunity,' as described in the next chapter.

CHAPTER **9**.

4. **nominum error**, 'uncertainty about the names,' **262** (*a*). **utrius—fuerint**, indirect question, **420**.

9. **vicissent**, subjunctive due to virtual *oratio obliqua*.

14. **animo**, ablative of place. Translate:—'Their minds are on the stretch with excitement and anxiety.'

16. **animos**, 'spirit,' 'courage,' as often in the plural.

25. **ut segregaret—capessit.** For this sequence after the historic present see **411** (note).

26. **aliquantum.** For this accusative compare c. 8, l. 9.

30. **dum—inclamat.** See **338**.

31. **Horatius,** 'the surviving Horatius.'

36. **Marte,** 'battle.' So *Venus* is used for 'love.'

38. **geminata victoria ferox,** 'exulting in his double victory.' Compare c. 3, l. 8 *ferox viribus.*

44. **eo—fuerat,** 'with all the greater joy, the nearer their fortunes had been to disaster.' *eo—quo,* ablatives of measure, **244.**

46. **alteri—alteri.** See **327** (note).

CHAPTER 10.

3. **portam Capenam.** See Plan of Rome.

7. **ferocis iuvenis,** 'of the triumphant warrior.' Compare c. 9, l. 38.

12. **sic eat.** Compare c. 2, l. 18 *sic pereat.*

15. **meritum,** 'service,' not 'merit.'

facto obstabat, 'was a set-off against his crime.'

16. **auctore Tullo.** Compare c. 8, l. 7.

18. **de provocatione—ad populum,** 'the question of the appeal was fought before the public assembly.'

22. **huncine,** for *hunce* 'this man here'+enclitic *ne.* See **96** (*d*).

24. **lictor.** See note on c. 16, l. 1.

25. **paulo,** ablative of measure, **244.**

30. **ipsius,** 'of the hero himself.'

CHAPTER 11.

2. **quod—fuerit,** giving the reason for the *invidia vulgi.* Hence the subjunctive, due to virtual *oratio obliqua.*

4. **per speciem societatis,** 'under the guise of alliance.' For *per* denoting manner compare c. 5, l. 2 *per iram.*

6. **Veientibus,** 'men of Veii,' in Etruria. See Map.

7. **Fidenae,** in Latium. See Map.

18. **gratulor** here takes dative of person and accusative of thing; for *devictos hostes* means 'conquest of his foes,' **393.**

22. **quod,** referring to what follows. Translate it by 'my design.'

sit, subjunctive expressing a wish.

24. **ad haec,** 'at these words.'

37. **ad diruendam urbem.** Compare c. 4, l. 25, c. 5, l. 26.

41.. **templis—temperatum est.** See 302.

43. **Caelius mons.** See Plan of Rome.

CHAPTER 12.

3. **patres fuere auctores,** 'the elders (the Senate) were approvers,' *i.e.* 'they gave their *auctoritas* (approval).'

4. **civibus—facta spes,** 'the citizens conceived the hope,' 222.

10. **desidem,** predicative. Translate:—'They thought that the King of Rome would spend his reign lazily amid shrines and altars.'

17. **Palatium.** See c. 3, l. 1.

18. **Capitolium atque arcem,** the two summits of the Capitoline Hill. See Plan.

20. **Ianiculum,** a hill on the west bank of the Tiber, marked in the Plan.

21. **ponte Sublicio,** 'the Bridge of Piles' (*sublicae*). Compare c. 13, l. 44.

22. **Quiritium.** See c. 6, l. 23.

25. **foro,** the 'market-place,' or great square of Rome. See Plan.

26. **hoc rege.** See § 237.

silva Mesia, a forest near Veii.

28. **Ostia** means 'the town at the mouth.'

29. **salinae.** The position of the Salt-works is given in the Map.

30. **Lucumo,** Etruscan prince or noble, in the Etruscan language *lauchme.*

32. **Tarquiniis,** 'at Tarquinii,' a city in Etruria.

peregrinus. His father Demaratus had come as an exile from Corinth.

40. **esset,** because the clause is in *oratio obliqua.*

43. **ventum erat.** See 301.

44. **demissa,** 'descending.'

46. **capiti,** dative similar to that after verbs of *giving.*

49. **excelsa,** 'majestic things.'

51. **L.** *i.e.* Lucius, as the nearest Roman name in sound to Lucumo.

Priscus, 'the Elder.'

54. **consiliis.** See **220** (*b*).

militiae domique, old locatives, **272** (*a*). Compare c. 3, l. 19.

CHAPTER **13.**

3. **eo magis—fierent,** 'so Tarquinius was all the more urgent that the assembly for the appointment of a king should be held as early as possible.'

5. **regi creando.** See **380.**

quibus indictis, 'and, when notice of this meeting had been given...'

sub tempus, 'close up to the time,' 'just before.' Compare *sub noctem* 'at nightfall.'

6. **venatum.** See **386.**

12. **circo, qui nunc maximus dicitur.** See Plan of Rome.

14. **cum—intervenit.** For the 'inverse *cum*' see **434.**

16. **Aniēnem.** The Anio is a tributary of the Tiber. See Map.

18. **trepidatum est,** 'a panic arose.' Compare c. 5, l. 14.

dubia victoria—magna caede. Distinguish between these ablatives. The first is absolute, the second denotes manner.

22. **equitem—viribus,** 'that his forces were specially weak in cavalry.'

23. **negat—favissent.** In *oratio recta* this would be *hoc fieri non potest, nisi—faverint.*

25. **age—divine tu.** 'Come, prophetic sir.' For this meaning of *divinus* compare Milton, 'Adam, whose heart, divine of something ill...'

33. **comitio,** 'meeting-place' of the popular assembly, adjoining the Forum. See Plan.

35. **certe,** 'anyhow,' *i.e.* whether the story is true or false.

36. **belli domique.** Compare c. 12, l. 54 *militiae domique*.

37. **concilia—dirimerentur,** '(and that) assemblies of the people and armies when summoned were broken up, whenever the omens were unfavourable.'

38. **admisissent,** subjunctive due to virtual *oratio obliqua*.

39. **iterum—confligitur,** 'there is a second collision with the Sabines.' Compare l. 18.

41. **vim lignorum.** So Virgil has *canum vis* 'a pack of hounds.'

51. **Latinis,** dative of disadvantage.

52. **omne nomen Latinum,** *i.e.* all the population of Latium.

CHAPTER 14.

2. **puero,** dative of possessor.

cui Servio Tullio fuit nomen. The attraction is illustrated in 224 (note).

10. **viden,** contracted for *videsne*.

15. **quod diis cordi est,** 'what the gods have *at heart*.' **cordi** is the locative case like *animi, domi, belli, militiae, Romae*, which we have had above.

16. **indolis regiae,** genitive of quality, 255.

17. **Tarquinio,** dative of advantage, not agent.

18. **tantus honos habitus,** 'the rendering of such high honour.' See 393.

19. **parvum,** 'when a child.'

CHAPTER 15.

13. **vociferari—obstrepere,** historic infinitives, as often in vivid descriptions.

16. **dum—avertit.** Compare c. 9, l. 30.

18. **deiecit,** 'brought down heavily.'

23. **Servio—accito,** not ablative absolute, but dative after *ostendisset*.

32. **et nos,** 'we also.'

38. **bono animo,** ablative of quality,—'of good courage.'

41. **omnia salubria esse,** 'that all the symptoms were favourable.'

CHAPTER 16.

1. **trabea,** the royal robe, striped with purple and white.

lictoribus. The lictors were attendants on the King; they carried the *fasces*, *i.e.* a bundle of rods with an axe; and scourged or beheaded condemned criminals.

5. **palam factum est,** ' the truth was made clear.'

15. **ut Servium—ferant,** consecutive clause, **421:**—' so that posterity (or 'history,' as we might say) extols Servius as the originator of all ranks and gradations of dignity in the state.'

16. **censum,** ' the register' of citizens and their property.

17. **rem—imperio,** 'a most salutary institution for an empire destined to be so great.'

18. **ex quo—fierent,** final clause:—'so that on the basis of this register the duties of war and peace might be performed in proportion to each man's wealth.' For instance, in the military arrangement of Servius the rich had to provide themselves with full and good armour, while the poor fought only with darts and slings.

19. **classes.** These classes were five in number, arranged *ex censu* ' according to the register,' *i.e.* according to property.

centurias. Each class was divided into so many 'centuries' (divisions of a hundred).

21. **urbs—visa est,** 'Servius thought that the city also ought to be enlarged.'

22. **Quirinalem Viminalemque.** The Quirinal and Viminal are the two most northerly of the Seven Hills.

23. **Esquiliis,** ablative of measure:—'he increases Rome by the Esquiliae' (literally 'the outside dwellings'), *i.e.* the Esquiline quarter. See Plan.

24. **aggere.** 'The mound of Servius Tullius' was a great rampart, on some of the highest ground in Rome, stretching from the southern side of the Esquiline to the northern side of the Quirinal.

muro. 'The Walls of Servius,' denoted by a thick line in the Plan, continued to be the walls of Rome for nearly eight hundred years.

26. **ita ut—esset,** 'so well that even a good and temperate successor would have found it hard to rival him.'

27. **id—occiderunt,** 'this also was added to his glory, that along with him just and lawful rule came to an end.'

32. **liberandae patriae,** objective genitive, depending on *consilia,* **262** (*a*).

CHAPTER **17.**

2. **Tulliae,** wife of Tarquinius Superbus.

8. **monumentoque locus est,** 'and the place serves as a memorial,' literally 'is *for a memorial,*' **225.**

9. **Sceleratum vicum vocant,** 'they call it the Street of Crime.'

13. **cui Superbo cognomen facta dederunt.** For the attraction compare c. 14, l. 2, *cui Servio Tullio fuit nomen.* **Superbus** means 'the Tyrant.'

21. **iniussu.** Compare l. 2, *iussu* and see **65.**

24. **Iovis templum,** on the Capitoline Hill. The Temple is marked in the Plan.

27. **caput humanum.** The story is meant to give the origin of the name of the hill.

integra facie, 'with the face well-preserved,' ablative of quality.

29. **haud per ambages,** 'not in a riddle,' 'straightforwardly.'

32. **operis,** 'gangs of workmen.' See **61.**

CHAPTER **18.**

1. **Gabios.** See Map.

8. **praedatum.** Cf. c. 13, 6, *venatum,* and l. 16 below.

17. **dubiae fidei,** genitive of quality.

23. **ut re imperfecta,** 'thinking that his errand had failed.'

25. **emisisse,** depending on *dicit* to be understood out of *refert.*

26. **quid parens—ambagibus,** 'the instructions his father meant to give by his dumb show.'

CHAPTER 19.

4. **ad publica—adhiberentur,** 'were usually called in to consider prodigies affecting the state.'

6. **Delphos,** a city in Phocis, celebrated for its temple and oracle of Apollo.

12. **iuvenis—induerat,** 'a youth far different in character from that of which he had assumed the semblance.'

13. **ex industria—stultitiae,** 'purposely made up on the model of stupidity.'

14. **praedae esse regi.** See 225, and compare c. 17, l. 8, *monumento locus est.*

15. **Bruti.** The adjective *brutus* means 'lumpish,' 'dull.'

16. **liberator ille—animus,** 'that great spirit bent on delivering the people of Rome.'

17. **tempora.** This plural is often used for 'opportunity' or 'crisis.'

21. **sciscitantur—esset venturum.** See 411 (note).

22. **ex infimo specu.** In the innermost sanctuary of the temple at Delphi there was a cleft in the ground, from which arose vapours with the power of producing ecstasy. Over the cleft was the seat of the prophetess, called Pythia. When she prophesied, no one was present but a priest, who afterwards explained to those who came to consult the oracle the words she uttered in her ecstasy.

25. **uter—daret.** The direct question to be decided would be :—*uter prior, cum Romam redierimus, matri osculum dabit?*

27. **alio—vocem,** literally 'that the words of the Pythia looked in another direction,' *i.e.* 'had another reference.'

30. **reditum.** Compare l. 20 *ventum est.*

CHAPTER 20.

3. **eius ingenii.** Cf. c. 18, l. 17.

5. **cloacas.** Considerable remains of the vast drainage system, due to the later kings, still exist.

9. **regi,** dative of disadvantage; so also l. 18 *Tarquinio.*

12. **Ardeam.** See Map.

21.   **exulatum.**   See **128.**
24.   **veterum simultatium.**   See c. 18.
26.   **ab condita urbe ad liberatam.**   See **393**.
27.   **annos ducentos quadraginta quattuor.**   See page xv.
duo consules.   The one life-king is superseded by two year-kings.   A return to tyranny is prevented by the annual and joint tenure of the regal *imperium.*   *consules* means strictly 'colleagues.'
28.   **creati sunt,** by the assembly of the people.
29.   **Collatinus,** ' of Collatia,' a Sabine town.

VOCABULARY.

ABBREVIATIONS.

abl.	ablative.	n.	neuter.
acc.	accusative.	neg.	negative.
adj.	adjective.	part.	participle.
adv.	adverb.	pers.	person, personal.
comp.	comparative.	pf.	perfect.
conj.	conjunction.	pl.	plural.
def.	defective.	poss.	possessive.
demonstr.	demonstrative.	prep.	preposition.
dep.	deponent.	pron.	pronoun.
f.	feminine.	rel.	relative.
gen.	genitive.	sing.	singular.
impers.	impersonal.	superl.	superlative.
indecl.	indeclinable.	v.a.	verb active.
indef.	indefinite.	v.n.	verb neuter.
inter.	interrogative.	1, 2, 3, 4	1st, 2nd, 3rd, 4th conjugation.
irreg.	irregular.		
m.	masculine.		

ā and ab, prep. with abl. *by, from.*

abdūcō, -ere, -xī, -ctum, 3 v.a. *lead away.*

abhorreō, -ēre, -uī, 2 v.n. *be remote from, be unlike.*

abigō, -ere, -ēgī, -actum, 3 v.a. *drive away.*

abnuō, -ere, -uī, 3 v.a. and n. *refuse.*

abrogō, -āre, āvī, -ātum, 1 v.a. *annul*

absens, gen. -entis, *absent.*

absolvō, -ere, -lvī, -lūtum, 3 v.a. *acquit.*

abstergeō, -ēre, -rsī, -rsum, 2 v.a. *wipe off.*

absum, -esse, -fuī, irreg. v.n. *be absent, be distant.*

ac, conj. *and*

accēdō, -ere, -cessī, -cessum, 3 v.n. *come to, be added.*

accendō, -ere, -ndī, -nsum, 3 v.a. *kindle.*

acciō, -cīre, -cīvī, -cītum, 4 v.a. *summon.*

accipiō, -ere, -cēpī, -ceptum, 3 v.a. *receive*; pf. part. **acceptus,** *accepted, acceptable.*

accola, -ae, m. *neighbour.*

ācer, -cris, -cre, *sharp, keen.*

aciēs, -eī, f. *line of battle.*

ācriter, adv. *keenly.* **ācrius,** *more keenly.* **ācerrimē,** *most keenly.*

ad, prep. with acc. *to.*

adaequō, -āre, -āvī, -ātum, 1 v.a. *level with.*

addō, -ere, -didī, -ditum, 3 v.a. *add.*

adeō, adv. *to such an extent, so much.*

adeō, -īre, -īvī or -iī, -itum, 4 v.n. *go to, approach.*

adhibeō, -ēre, -uī, -itum, 2 v.a. *apply, call in.*

adiciō, -ere, -iēcī, -iectum, 3 v.a. *add.*

adimō, -ere, -ēmī, -emptum, 3 v.a. *take away.*

adipiscor, -scī, adeptus sum, 3 dep. v.a. *obtain.*

adiungō, -ere, -nxī, -nctum, 3 v.a. *join to.*

adiuvō, -āre, -iūvī, -iūtum, 1 v.a. *help.*

administrō, -āre, -āvī, -ātum, 1 v.a. *administer, manage.*

admīrātiō, -ōnis, f. *admiration, wonder.*

admittō, -ere, -mīsī, -missum, 3 v.a. *admit, allow.*

admoveō, -ēre, -vī, -tum, 2 v.a. *move to.*

adolescens, -ntis, m. *young man.*

adolescō, -ere, -olēvī, -ultum, 3 v.n. *grow up*; pf. part. **adultus**, *grown up.*

adorior, -īrī, -ortus sum, 4 dep. v.n. *attack.*

adstō, -stitī, 1 v.n. *stand by.*

adsum, -esse, -fuī, irreg. v.n. *be present.*

adsūmō, -ere, -sumpsī, -sumptum, 3 v.a. *take to one-self.*

advena, -ae, m. *foreigner.*

adversus, prep. with acc. *a-gainst.*

aedēs, -is, f. sing. *temple*; pl. *house.*

aedificō, -āre, -āvī, -ātum, 1 v.a. *build.*

aegrē, adv. *ill.*

aemulātiō, -ōnis, f. *rivalry.*

aequō, -āre, -āvī, -ātum, 1 v.a. *make equal, level.*

aetās, -ātis, f. *age.*

afferō, -ferre, attulī, allātum, irreg. v.a. *bring to.*

affīnitās, -ātis, f. *connexion by marriage.*

affirmō, -āre, -āvī, -ātum, 1 v.a. and n. *affirm.*

affligō, -ere, -ixī, -ictum, 3 v.a. *damage, afflict.*

ager, agrī, m. *field, territory.*

agger, -eris, m. *mound.*

aggredior, -ī, -gressus sum, 3 dep. v.a. *approach, attack.*

agitō, -āre, -āvī, -ātum, 1 v.a. *drive, hunt, ponder.*

agō, -ere, ēgī, actum, 3 v.a. and n. *do, act, conduct, drive.*

agrestis, -e, *rustic.*

āiō, def. v.a. and n. *say.*

ālea, -ae, f. *hazard.*

aliēnus, -a, -um, *belonging to another.*

aliō, adv. *in another direction.*

aliquantum, -ī, n. *some a-mount.*

aliquis, -id, indef. pron. *some, some one.*

aliquot, indef. num. indecl. *some, several.*

alius, -a, -ud, adj. *other.*

alliciō, -ere, -lexī, -lectum, 3 v.a. *entice.*

alloquor, -quī, -cūtus sum, 3 dep. v.a. *address.*

alō, -ere, -uī, -itum, 3 v.a. *nourish.*

alter, -era, -erum, adj. *one of two, other of two.*

altus, -a, -um, *high, deep*; adv. **altē**, *high, deep.*

alveus, -ī, m. *trough.*

ambāgēs, -ium, f. pl. *riddle, dumb show.*

ambitiōsē, adv. *by courting popularity.*

ambō, -ae, -o, *both.*

āmens, -ntis, adj. *mad.*

amīcitia, -ae, f. *friendship.*

amīcus, -ī, m. *friend.*

āmittō, -ere, -mīsī, -missum,
3 v.a. *lose.*
amo, -āre, -āvī, -ātum, 1 v.a.
love.
amor, -ōris, m. *love.*
amplector, -ctī, -xus sum, 3
dep. v.a. *embrace.*
amplificō, -āre, -āvī, -ātum,
1 v.a. *enlarge.*
an, conj. *whether, or.*
anceps, -cipitis, adj. *doubtful.*
anguis, -is, m. and f. *snake.*
animus, -ī, m. *mind, courage.*
annus, -ī, m. *year.*
ante, prep. with acc. *before* ;
adv. *before.*
ānulus, -ī, m. *ring.*
anxius, -a, -um, *anxious.*
aperiō, -īre, -uī, -rtum, 4 v.a.
open. apertē, adv. *openly.*
appāreō, -ēre, -uī, -itum, 2
v.n. *appear.*
appāritor, -oris, m. *attendant.*
appellō, -āre, -āvī, -ātum, 1
v.a. *call, appeal to.*
aptē, adv. *fitly, neatly.*
apud, prep. w. acc. *at, among,
with.*
aqua, -ae, f. *water.*
aquila, -ae, f. *eagle.*
āra, -ae, f. *altar.*
arbitror, -ārī, -ātus sum, 1
dep. v.n. *think.*
arbor, -ōris, f. *tree.*
arceō, -ēre, -cuī, 2 v.a. *keep off.*
ardeō, -ēre, -sī, -sum, 2 v.n.
burn.
argentum, -ī, n. *silver.*
arguō, -ere, -uī, ūtum, 3 v.a.
urge, accuse.
arma, -ōrum, n. pl. *arms.*
armentum, -ī, n. *herd.*
armilla, -ae, f. *bracelet.*
armō, -āre, -āvī, -ātum, 1 v.a.
arm.
ars, artis, f. *art, accomplish-
ment, artifice.*

arx, arcis, f. *citadel.*
ascendō, -ere, -ndī, -nsum,
3 v.a. *ascend.*
aspiciō, -ere, -spexī, -spectum,
3 v.a. *behold.*
astō, -āre, astitī, 1 v.n. *stand
by, stand still.*
asȳlum, -ī, n. *asylum.*
at, conj. *but, yet.*
atque, conj. *and.*
atquī, conj. *but.*
atrox, -ōcis, adj. *savage,
cruel.*
auctor, -ōris, m. *author, ad-
viser, supporter.*
audācia, -ae, f. *audacity, bold-
ness.*
audeō, -ēre, ausus sum, 2
semi-dep. v.n. *dare.*
audiō, -īre, -īvī, -ītum, 4 v.a.
hear.
auferō,-ferre,abstulī,ablātum,
irreg. v.a. *take away.*
aufugiō, -ere, -fūgī, -fugitum,
3 v.n. *flee away, escape.*
augeō, -ēre, auxī, auctum, 2
v.a. *increase.*
augur, -uris, m. *augur, soothsayer.*
augurium, -ī, n. *augury, di-
vination.*
aureus, -a, -um, adj. *golden.*
auspicātō, adv. *with good
omens.*
aut, conj. *either, or.*
autem, conj. *but.*
auxilium, -ī, n. *help.*
āvertō, -ere, -tī, -sum, 3 v.a.
turn away, drive off, steal.
avidus, -a, -um, *greedy.*
avis, -is, f. *bird.*
avus, -ī, m. *grandfather.*

baculum, -ī, n. *staff.*
bellātor, -oris, m. *warrior.*
bellō, -āre, -āvī, -ātum, 1 v.n.
wage war.

44   *The Story of the Kings*

bellum, -ī, n. *war.*

benignē, adv. *kindly.*

bona, -ōrum, n. pl. *goods.*

bonus, -a, -um, *good.*

bos, bovis, m. and f. *ox, cow.*

bracchium, -ī, n. *arm.*

brevis, -e, *short.*

cadō, -ere,cecidī, cāsum, 3 v.n. *fall.*

caecus, -a, -um, *blind.*

caedēs, -is, f. *slaughter.*

caedō, -ere, cecīdī, caesum, 3 v.a. *strike, kill.*

caelestis, -e, *heavenly.*

caelum, -ī, n. *sky.*

campus, -ī, m. *plain.*

capessō, -ere, 3 v.a. *lay hold of, have recourse to.*

capiō, -ere, cēpī, captum, 3 v.a. *take, seize, captivate.*

caput, -itis, n. *head.*

carcer, -eris, m. *prison.*

cāritās, -tātis, f. *affection.*

carpentum, -ī, n. *chariot.*

castra, -orum, n. pl. *camp.*

cauda, -ae, f. *tail.*

causa, -ae, f. *cause, reason.*

cēdō, -ere, cessī, cessum, 3 v.a. and n. *yield.*

cēlō, -āre, -āvī, -ātum, 1 v.a. *conceal.*

census, -ūs, m. *census, rating.*

centum, indecl. num. *hundred.*

centuria, -ae, f. *division of a hundred men, century.*

centuriō, -ōnis, m. *centurion.*

certāmen, -inis, n. *contest.*

certātim, adv. *in rivalry.*

certō, -āre, -āvī, -ātum, 1 v.n. *strive.*

certus, -a, -um, *certain*; adv. certē, *certainly.*

cēterus, -a, -um, *the rest.*

cibus, -ī, m. *food.*

circā, prep. w. acc., and adv. *around.*

circumdō, -are, -dedī, -datum, 1 v.a. *surround.*

circumferō, -ferre, -tulī, -lātum, irreg. v.a. *carry round.*

circumfundō, -ere, -fūdī, -fūsum, 3 v.a. *pour round.*

circumsistō, -ere, -stetī, 3 v.n. *stand round.*

circumstō, -āre, -stetī, 1 v.n. *stand round.*

circus, -ī, m. *circus.*

citō, adv. *quickly.*

cīvis, -is, m. *citizen.*

cīvitās, -ātis, f. *state, community.*

clam, adv. *secretly.*

clāmitō,-āre,-āvī,-ātum,1v.a. *keep crying out.*

clāmor, -ōris, m. *shout.*

clangor, -ōris, m. *noise, cry.*

clārus, -a, -um, *distinguished, famous.*

classis, -is, f. *class, fleet.*

claudō, -ere, -sī, -sum, 3 v.a. *shut.*

clāva, -ae, f. *club.*

clēmens, -ntis, adj. *clement, merciful.*

cloāca, -ae, f. *sewer.*

coepī, -isse, coeptus sum, def. v.a. and n. *begin.*

coeptum, -ī, n. *undertaking.*

coerceō, -ēre, -cuī, -citum, 2 v.a. *confine, restrain.*

cōgitō, -āre, -āvī, -ātum, 1 v.a. *think.*

cognātus, -a, -um, *related.*

cognōmen, -inis, n. *surname.*

cognoscō,ᵣere,-gnōvī,-gnitum, 3 v.a. *perceive, know.*

cōgō, -ere, coēgī, coactum, 3 v.a. *force.*

colligō,-āre,-āvī,-ātum,1v.a. *bind together.*

colligō, -ere, -lēgī, -lectum, 3 v.a. *collect.*

colloquium, -ī, n.*conversation.*

Vocabulary 45

colō, -ere, -uī, cultum, 3 v.a. *cultivate, worship.*
colōnia, -ae, f. *colony.*
columna, -ae, f. *column, pillar.*
comes, -itis, m. *companion.*
comitium, -iī, n. *meeting-place,* pl. *meeting, assembly.*
commentum, -ī, n. *pretence.*
committō, -ere, -mīsī, -missum, 3 v.a. *commit, entrust.*
commodum, -ī, n. *convenience.*
commūnis, -e, *common, joint.*
commūniter, adv. *jointly.*
compellō, -ere, pulī, -pulsum, 3 v.a. *drive together.*
complector, -ī, -plexus sum, 3 dep. v.a. *embrace.*
complōrātiō, -ōnis, f. *lamentation.*
compositus, -a, -um, pf. part. of compōnō, *arranged*; ex compositō, *by arrangement.*
comprehendō, -ere, -dī, -prehensum or -prensum, 3 v.a. *seize, arrest.*
comprimō, -ere, -pressī, -pressum, 3 v.a. *check.*
cōnātus, -ūs, m. *attempt.*
conciliō, -āre, -āvī, -ātum, 1 v.a. *conciliate, win over.*
concilium, -ī, n. *council, meeting.*
concipiō, -ere, -cēpī, -ceptum, 3 v.a. *conceive.*
concitō, -āre, -āvī, -ātum, 1 v.a. *incite.*
conclāmō, -āre, -āvī, -ātum, 1 v.a. *shout together.*
concurrō, -ere, -currī, -cursum, 3 v.n. *run together, charge.*
concursus, -ūs, m. *running together, charge.*
conditor, -ōris, m. *founder, builder.*
condō, -ere, -didī, -ditum, 3 v.a. *found, build.*

conferō, -ferre, -tulī, collātum, irreg. v.a. *bring together.*
conficiō, -ere, -fēcī, -fectum, 3 v.a. *complete, make, finish off.*
confirmō, -āre, -āvī, -ātum, 1 v.a. *confirm, strengthen.*
confīgō, -ere, -xī, -ctum, 3 v.n. *clash, contend.*
congredior, -ī, -gressus sum, 3 dep. v.n. *come together, meet.*
congregō, -āre, -āvī, -ātum, 1 v.a. *gather together.*
congressus, -ūs, m. *meeting.*
coniciō, -ere, -iēcī, -iectum, 3 v.a. *throw.*
coniungō, -ere, -nxī, -nctum, 3 v.a. *join.*
coniux, -ugis, m. and f. *husband, wife.*
cōnor, -ārī, -ātus sum, 1 dep. v.a. *attempt.*
conqueror, -ī, -questus sum, 3 dep. v.n. *complain bitterly.*
conscrībō, -ere, -psī, -ptum, 3 v.a. *enlist, levy.*
consensus, -ūs, m. *agreement, harmony.*
consequor, -ī, -secūtus sum, 3 dep. v.a. *follow up, overtake.*
consīdō, -ere, -sēdī, -sessum, 3 v.n. *sit down, encamp.*
consilium, -ī, n. *counsel, policy, body of advisers.*
consociō, -āre, -āvī, -ātum, 1 v.a. *unite.*
conspectus, -ūs, m. *sight.*
conspiciō, -ere, -spexī, -spectum, 3 v.a. *see, catch sight of.*
constituō, -ere, -uī, -ūtum, 3 v.a. *arrange, determine.*
constō, -āre, -stitī, 1 v.n. *be settled, be agreed.*
consul, -ulis, m. *consul.*
consulō, -ere, -uī, -ultum, 3 v.a. *consult.*

consultus, -a, -um, *skilled.*

contentus, -a, -um, *content.*

contingō, -ere, -tigī, -tactum, 3 v.a. and n. *touch, happen.*

contiō, -ōnis, f. *meeting.*

contrā, prep. with acc. *against;* adv. *opposite.*

contumēlia, -ae, f. *abuse, reproach.*

cōnūbium, -ī, n. *marriage.*

convertō, -ere, -tī, -sum, 3 v.a. *turn.*

coorior, -īrī, -ortus sum, 4 dep. v.n. *arise.*

cōpia, -ae, f. *plenty;* plur. *forces, troops.*

cor, cordis, n. *heart.*

cornū, -ūs, n. *horn, wing (of army).*

corpus, -oris, n. *body.*

corrumpō, -ere, -rūpī, -ruptum, 3 v.a. *corrupt, spoil, bribe.*

corruō, -ere, -ruī, 3 v.n. *collapse.*

cōs, cōtis, f. *whetstone.*

crēdō, -ere, -didī, -ditum, 3 v.a. and n. *believe.*

creō, -āre, -āvī, -ātum, 1 v.a. *create, make, appoint.*

crescō, -ere, crēvī, crētum, 3 v.n. *increase.*

crīnis, -is, m. *hair;* mostly pl.

cruciātus, -ūs, m. *torture.*

crūdēlis, -e, *cruel.*

cruor, -ōris, m. *blood.*

cultus, -ūs, m. *cultivation, training, style.*

cum, prep. with abl. *with.*

cum, conj. *when, since.*

cunctanter, adv. *with delay.*

cunctor, -ārī, -ātus sum, 1 dep. v.n. *delay.*

cupidus, -a, -um, *desirous, eager.*

cupiō, -ere, -īvī or -iī, -ītum, 3 v.a. *desire.*

cūr, adv. *why.*

cūra, -ae, f. *care.*

cūria, -ae, f. *senate-house.*

currō, -ere, cucurrī, cursum, 3 v.n. *run.*

cursus, -ūs, m. *running, course.*

custōdia, -ae, f. *imprisonment, prison.*

dē, prep. w. abl. *down from. concerning.*

dea, -ae, f. *goddess.*

decem, indecl. *ten.*

dēcernō, -ere, -crēvī, -crētum, 3 v.a. *decide, decree.*

dēcipiō, -ere, -cēpī, -ceptum, 3 v.a. *deceive.*

dēclārō, -āre, -āvī, -ātum, 1 v.a. *declare, make clear.*

decus, -oris, n. *glory, honour.*

dēcutiō, -ere, -cussī, -cussum, 3 v.a. *strike down.*

dēdecus, -oris, n. *disgrace.*

dēdō, -ere, dēdidī, dēditum, 3 v.a. *yield.*

dēdūcō, -ere, -xī, -ctum, 3 v.a. *lead down, conduct.*

dēferō, -ferre, -tulī, -latum, irreg. v.a. *carry down, offer.*

dēfīgō, -ere, -xī, -xum, 3 v.a. *fix down, plant.*

dēfungor, -ī, -functus sum, 3 dep. v.a. *finish off.*

dēiciō, -ere, -iēcī, -iectum, 3 v.a. *throw down.*

dein, and deinde, *then, next.*

deinceps, adv. *in succession, next.*

dēlābor, -ī, lapsus sum, 3 v.n. *glide down, descend.*

dēleō, -ēre, -ēvī, -ētum, 2 v.a. *blot out.*

dēlīberābundus, -a, -um, *deliberating.*

dēligō, -ere, -lēgī, -lectum, 3 v.a. *pick out, select.*

dēmergō, -ere, -sī, -sum, 3 v.a.
submerge, bury.
dēmittō, -ere, -misī, -missum,
3 v.a. *send down.*
dēmum, adv. *at length.*
densus, -a, -um, *thick.*
dēpōnō, -ere, -posuī,-positum,
3 v.a. *put down, resign.*
dēposcō, -ere, -poposcī, 3 v.a.
demand.
dēscendō,-ere,-dī,-sum,3 v.n.
go down, descend.
dēsciscō, -ere, -scīvī, -scītum,
3 v.n. *withdraw, revolt.*
dēscrībō, -ere, -psī, -ptum, 3
v.a. *mark out, define.*
dēserō,-ere,-ruī,-rtum, 3 v.a.
desert.
dēses, -idis, adj. *idle.*
dēsīderium, -ī, n. *regret, long-
ing.*
dēsignō, -āre, -āvī, -ātum, 1
v.a. *mark out, designate.*
dēsistō, -ere, -stitī, 3 v.n.
leave off, desist.
dēspondeō, -ēre, -dī, -sum, 2
v.a. *betroth.*
dēstituō, -ere, -uī, -ūtum, 3
v.a. *desert, leave.*
dēsum, -esse, -fuī, irreg. v.n.
be wanting, fail.
deus, -ī, m. *god.*
dēvincō, -ere, -vīcī, -victum,
3 v.a. *conquer completely.*
dextra, -ae, f. *right hand.*
diciō, -ōnis, f. *sway, rule.*
dīcō, -ere, -xī, -ctum, 3 v.a.
and n. *say, call.*
dictātor, -ōris, m. *dictator,
commander.*
dictitō,-āre,-āvī,-ātum,1 v.n.
say often, assert.
dies, -eī, m. and f. in sing., m.
in pl. *day.*
dignitās, -ātis, f. *dignity,
rank.*
dignus, -a, -um, *worthy.*

dīmicātiō, -ōnis, f. *struggle.*
dīmicō, -āre,-āvī,-ātum, 1 v.n.
fight it out.
dīrimō, -ere, -ēmī, -emptum,
3 v.a. *separate, break up.*
dīruō, -ere, -ruī, -rutum, 3 v.a.
demolish.
discerpō, -ere, -psī, -ptum, 3
v.a. *tear in pieces.*
discindō, -ere, -cidī, -cissum,
3 v.a. *cleave.*
discrīmen, -inis, n. *difference,
danger.*
discurrō,-ere,-currī,-cursum,
3 v.n. *run in different direc-
tions.*
dispār, -paris, adj. *unlike.*
displiceō, -ēre, -uī, -itum, 2
v.n. *displease.*
dissimilis, -e, *unlike.*
distrahō,-ere,-xī,-ctum,3 v.a.
drag apart, tear asunder.
diū, adv. *long*; comp. diūtius.
dīversus, -a, -um, *different.*
dīvidō, -ere, -vidī, -vīsum, 3
v.a. *divide.*
dīvīnus, -a, -um, *divine, prophetic.*
dīvitiae, -ārum, f. *riches.*
dō, dare, dedī, datum, 1 v.a.
give, afford, place, cause.
doceō, -ēre, -cuī, -ctum, 2 v.a.
teach, show.
dolus, -ī, m. *craft, trick.*
domesticus, -a, -um, *domes-
tic.*
domina, -ae, f. *mistress.*
dominātiō, -ōnis, f. *tyranny.*
dominus, -ī, m. *lord, master.*
domō, -āre, -uī, -itum, 1 v.a.
tame, subdue.
domus, -ūs or -ī,f. *house, home*;
locative, domī, *at home.*
dōnec, conj. *until.*
dōnum, -ī, n. *gift.*
dormiō, -īre, -īvī, -ītum, 4 v.n.
sleep.

dubitō, -āre, -āvī, -ātum, 1 v.n. *doubt, hesitate.*

dubius, -a, -um, *doubtful.*

dubiē, adv. *doubtfully.*

dūcentī, -ae, -a, *two hundred.*

dūcō, -ere, -xī, -ctum, 3 v.a. *lead.*

dulcēdō, -inis, f. *sweetness, charm.*

dum, conj. *while, until.*

dummodō, conj. *provided only that.*

duo, -ae, -o, *two.*

duodecim, indecl. *twelve.*

duodēquadrāgēsimus, -a,-um, *thirty-eighth.*

duplex, gen. -icis, adj. *double.*

duplicō, -āre, -āvī, -ātum, 1 v.a. *double.*

dux, ducis, m. *leader, general.*

ē and ex, prep. with abl. *out of, from.*

ēdīcō, -ere, -xī, -ctum, 3 v.a. *publish.*

ēdō, -ere, -didī, -ditum, 3 v.a. *bring forth, utter.*

ēdūcō, -āre, -āvī, -ātum, 1 v.a. *bring up.*

efferō, efferre, extulī, ēlātum. irreg v.a. *carry out, raise up.*

efficiō, -ere, -fēcī, -fectum, 3 v.a. *cause.*

effugiō, -ere, -fūgī, 3 v.a. and n. *escape.*

effundō, -ere, -fūdī, -fūsum, 3 v.a. *pour out, spread.*

effūsē, adv. *in confusion.*

ego, gen. mei, pron. *I.*

ēgredior, -ī, -gressus sum, 3 dep. v.n. *go out.*

ēgregius, -a, -um, *remarkable, excellent.*

ēiciō, -ere, -iēcī, -iectum, 3 v.a. *cast out.*

ēlābor, -ī, -lapsus sum, 3 dep. v.n. *glide out.*

ēluviēs, -eī, f. *overflow.*

ēmittō, -ere, -mīsī, -missum, 3 v.a. *send out.*

enim, conj. *for.*

ēniteō, -ēre, -tuī, 2 v.n. *shine out.*

eō, adv. *thither, by that much.*

eō, īre, īvī or iī, itum, 4 v.n. *go.*

eques, -itis, m. *horseman;* sing. collective, *cavalry.*

equus, -ī, m. *horse.*

ērectus, -a, -um, *animated, on the alert.*

ergā, prep. with acc. *towards.*

ergō, adv. *therefore.*

ērigō, -ere, -rexī, -rectum, 3 v.a. *raise up, encourage.*

error, -ōris, m. *error, doubt.*

et, conj. *and, also, even.*

etiam, adv. *also, even.*

ēvādō, -ere, -sī, -sum, 3 v.n. *go out, turn out.*

ēveniō, -īre, -vēnī, -ventum, 4 v.n. *happen.*

ēventus, -ūs, m. *event, result.*

ēvocō, -āre, -āvī, -ātum, 1 v.a. *call out.*

ex, see ē.

excelsus, -a, -um, *lofty.*

excidium, -ī, n. *destruction.*

exciō, -īre, -cīvī, -cītum, 4 v.a *arouse.*

excipiō, -ere, -cēpī, -ceptum, 3 v.a. *receive, welcome.*

excitō, -āre, -āvī, -ātum, 1 v.a. *stir up.*

exercitus, -ūs, m. *army.*

exigō, -ere, -ēgī, -actum, 3 v.a. *drive out.*

exilium, -ī, n. *exile.*

eximius, -a, -um, *excellent.*

exinde, adv. *next, after that.*

expergiscor, -ī, -perrectus sum, 3 dep. v.n. *wake up.*

experior, -īrī, -pertus sum, 4 dep. v.a. *test, experience.*

expōnō, -ere, -posuī, -positum, 3 v.a. *expose.*
exposcō, -ere, -poposcī, 3 v.a. *demand, entreat.*
exsanguis, -e, *bloodless.*
expectō, -āre, -āvī, -ātum, 1 v.a. *wait for, expect.*
exspīrō, -āre, -āvī, -ātum, 1 v.a. and n. *breathe out, expire.*
exterreō, -ēre, -uī, -itum,2 v.a. *alarm.*
exul, -ulis, m. *exile.*
exulō, -āre, -āvī, -ātum, 1 v.n. *be banished, live in exile.*
exultō, -āre, -āvī, -ātum, 1 v.n. *exult.*

faber, -brī, m. *workman.*
facies, -eī, f. *face.*
facilis, -e, *easy* ; adv. facile, *easily.*
facinus, -oris, n. *crime.*
faciō, -ere, fēcī, factum, 3 v.a. *make, do.*
factum, -ī, n. *deed.*
facultās, -ātis, f. *opportunity.*
fallō, -ere, fefellī, falsum, 3 v.a. *deceive.*
falsus, -a, -um, *false.*
fāma, -ae, f. *report.*
familiāris, -e, *belonging to the household.*
fās, n. indecl. *lawful.*
faustus, -a, -um, *auspicious.*
faveō, -ēre, fāvī, fautum, 2 v.n. *favour, support.*
fēlix, -īcis, adj. *lucky, happy.*
fēmina, -ae, f. *woman.*
fenestra, -ae, f. *window.*
fera, -ae, f. *wild beast.*
ferē, adv. *generally, about.*
fermē, adv. *generally, about.*
ferō, ferre, tulī, lātum, irreg. v.a. *carry, bear, relate.*
ferox, -ōcis, *spirited, warlike, proud.*

ferrum, -ī, n. *iron, sword.*
ferus, -a, -um, *wild, fierce.*
fessus, -a, -um, *weary.*
festīnō, -āre, -āvī, -ātum, 1 v.a. and n. *hasten.*
fidēlis, -e, *faithful.*
fides, -eī, f. *faith, credit.*
fīdūcia, -ae, f. *confidence.*
fīdus, -a, -um, *faithful.*
fīlia, -ae, f. *daughter.*
fīlius, -ī, m. *son.*
fīnis, -is, m. and f. *end* ; pl. m. *borders, territory.*
fīnitimus, -a, -um, *bordering, neighbouring.*
fīō, fierī, factus sum, irreg. semi-dep. *become, be made.*
firmō, -āre, -āvī, -ātum, 1 v.a. *strengthen.*
flamma, -ae, f. *flame.*
flēbiliter, adv. *mournfully.*
flectō, -ere, flexī, flexum, 3 v.a. *bend, turn.*
flōreō, -ēre, -uī, 2 v.n. *flourish.*
fluitō, -āre, -āvī, -ātum, 1 v.n. *float.*
flūmen, -inis, n. *river, stream.*
fluvius, -ī, m. *river.*
foedus, -eris, n. *treaty.*
foedus, -a, -um, *foul, disgraceful*; adv. foedē, *disgracefully.*
forās, adv. *out of doors, outwards.*
forma, -ae, f. *form, beauty.*
forte, adv. *by chance.*
fortis, -e, *brave, strong.*
fortūna, -ae, f. *fortune.*
forum, -ī, n. *forum, marketplace.*
fossa, -ae, f. *ditch.*
fragor, -ōris, m. *crash, din.*
frangō, -ere, frēgī, fractum, 3 v.a. *break.*
frāter, -tris, m. *brother.*
frēnum, -ī, n. *bridle, rein*; pl. frēnī, m. or frēna, n.

frētus, -a, -um, *relying on.*
fuga, -ae, f. *flight.*
fugiō, -ere, fūgī, fugitum, 3 v.n. *flee.*
fugō, -āre, -āvī, -ātum, 1 v.a. *put to flight.*
fulgeō, -ēre, fulsī, 2 v.n. *shine.*
fundāmentum, -ī, n. *foundation.*
fundō, -ere, fūdī, fūsum, 3 v.a. *pour, rout.*
fungor, -ī, functus sum, 3 dep. v.a. *perform.*
furia, -ae, f. *fury.*
furca, -ae, f. *fork, gibbet.*
futūrus, -a, -um, fut. part. of sum, *about to be, future.*

gaudium, -ī, n. *joy.*
geminō, -āre, -āvī, -ātum, 1 v.a. *double.*
geminus, -a, -um, *double, twin.*
gemmātus, -a, -um, *jewelled.*
gener, -erī, m. *son-in-law.*
gens, -ntis, f. *family, race, tribe.*
genus, -eris, n. *race, kind.*
gerō, -ere, gessī, gestum, 3 v.a. *carry, carry on, wage.*
gignō, -ere, genuī, genitum, 3 v.a. *give birth to.*
gladius, -ī, m. *sword.*
glōria, -ae, f. *glory.*
gradus, -ūs, m. *step, rank.*
grātia, -ae, f. *favour.*
grātulor, -ārī, -ātus sum, 1 dep. v.a. *congratulate.*
gravis, -e, *heavy.*
gravō, -āre, -āvī, -ātum, 1 v.a. *weigh down.*
grex, gregis, m. *flock, herd.*

habeō, -ēre, -uī, -itum, 2 v.a. *have, hold, keep, exercise, render.*
habitō, -āre, -āvī, -ātum, 1 v.n. *dwell.*

haereō, -ēre, haesī, haesum, 2 v.n. *stick, cling.*
hasta, -ae, f. *spear.*
haud, adv. *not.*
herbidus, -a, -um, *grassy.*
hic, haec, hoc, demonstr. pron. *this.*
hīc, adv. *here.*
hinc, adv. *hence.*
hodiē, adv. *to-day.*
homō, -inis, m. *man, human being.*
honōrātus, -a, -um, *distinguished.*
honōs or honor, -ōris, m. *honour, distinction, office.*
hōra, -ae, f. *hour.*
horror, -ōris, m. *shivering, horror.*
hortor, -ārī, -ātus sum, 1 dep. v.a. *exhort.*
hortus, -ī, m. *garden.*
hospitāliter, adv. *hospitably.*
hospitium, -ī, n. *hospitality.*
hostis, -is, m. *enemy.*
hūc, adv. *hither.*
hūmānus, -a, -um, *human.*
humerus, -ī, m. *shoulder.*
humilis, -e, *lowly, humble.*

ibī or ibi, adv. *there, then.*
ictus, pf. part. of old verb īcō, *struck.*
ictus, -ūs, m. *blow.*
īdem, eadem, idem, *the same.*
igitur, adv. *therefore.*
ignis, -is, m. *fire.*
ignōtus, -a, -um, *unknown.*
ille, -a, -ud, demonstr. pron. *that, he.*
illigō, -āre, -āvī, -ātum, 1 v.a. *bind, hamper.*
illūc, adv. *thither.*
imitātiō, -ōnis, f. *imitation.*
immātūrus, -a, -um, *unripe, unseasonable.*

Vocabulary

immineō, -ēre, 2 v.n. *overhang, threaten.*

immortālis, -e, *immortal.*

immortālitās, -ātis, f. *immortality.*

impediō, -īre, -īvī, -ītum, 4 v.a. *hinder.*

imperfectus, -a, -um, *unfinished.*

imperitō, -āre, -āvī, -ātum, 1 v.n. *command.*

imperium, -ī, n. *command, supreme power, sovereignty, empire.*

imperō, -āre, -āvī, -ātum, 1 v.a. and n. *command.*

impetus, -ūs, m. *attack, rush, charge.*

impiger, -gra, -grum, *untiring, energetic.*

impius, -a, -um, *impious, unnatural.*

impleō, -ēre, -ēvī, -ētum, 2 v.a. *fill.*

impōnō, -ere, -posuī, -positum, 3 v.a. *place on.*

in, prep. with acc. *into, against*; with abl. *in.*

inambulō, -āre, -āvī, -ātum, 1 v.n. *walk about.*

incendō, -ere, -ndī, -nsum, 3 v.a. *set on fire, inflame.*

incertus, -a, -um, *uncertain.*

incitō, -āre, -āvī, -ātum, 1 v.a. *stir up, incite.*

inclāmō, -āre, -āvī, -ātum, 1 v.a. *call on.*

inclīnō, -āre, -āvī, -ātum, 1 v.a. *turn, incline.*

inclitus, -a, -um, *famous.*

incola, -ae, m. *inhabitant.*

incolumis, -e, *safe, unharmed.*

increpō, -āre, -puī, -pitum, 1 v.a. *sound, rattle, abuse.*

incursiō, -ōnis, f. *attack, charge.*

incūsō, -āre, -āvī, -ātum, 1 v.a. *blame, complain of.*

inde, adv. *thence, then, thereupon.*

indīcō, -ere, -xī, -ctum, 3 v.a. *proclaim.*

indignitās, -ātis, f. *indignity.*

indignus, -a, -um, *unworthy.*

indolēs, -is, f. *nature, character.*

indulgentia, -ae, f. *kindness, indulgence.*

induō, -ere, -uī, -ūtum, 3 v.a. *put on, assume.*

industria, -ae, f. *industry*; ex industriā, *on purpose.*

ineō, -īre, -īvī and iī, -itum, 4 v.a. *enter.*

inermis, -e, *unarmed.*

infēlix, -īcis, adj. *unlucky, accursed.*

infensus, -a, -um, *hostile.*

inferō, -ferre, -tulī, -lātum or illātum, irreg. v.a. *bring in.*

infestus, -a, -um, *hostile*; of weapons, *in rest, couched.*

infimus, -a, -um, *lowest.*

infit, def. v. *begins to speak.*

ingenitus, -a, -um, *inborn, innate.*

ingenium, -ī, n. *intelligence, nature.*

ingens, -ntis, adj. *great, huge.*

ingredior, -ī, -gressus sum, 3 dep. v.n. *enter, advance.*

inhibeō, -ēre, -uī, -itum, 2 v.a. *hold in.*

inhūmānus, -a, -um, *inhuman.*

iniciō, -ere, -iēcī, -iectum, 3 v.a. *throw on.*

iniūria, -ae, f. *injury, injustice, wrong.*

iniussū, m. only abl. *without command.*

inquam, -is, -it, def. v.a. and n. *say.*

insānābilis, -e, *incurable.*

insepultus, -a, -um, *unburied.*

4—2

insidiae, -ārum, f. *stratagem, ambush.*

insignis, -e, *remarkable.*

insitus, -a, -um, *inborn.*

inspiciō, -ere, -spexī,-spectum, 3 v.a. *look into.*

instituō, -ere, -uī, -ūtum, 3 v.a. *begin, establish.*

institūtum, -ī, n. *ordinance.*

instō, -āre, -stitī, 1 v.n. *press on.*

intactus, -a, -um, *untouched.*

integer, -gra, -grum, *untouched,whole,fresh* ; de integro, *anew.*

intellegō, -ere, -xī, -ctum, 3 v.a. *understand.*

intendō, -ere, -ndī, -ntum, 3 v.a. *stretch.*

intentus, -a,-um,*intent, eager.*

inter, prep. with acc. *among, between.*

interficiō, -ficere,-fēcī,-fectum, 3 v.a. *kill.*

interim, adv. *meanwhile.*

interimō, -ere, -ēmī, -emptum, 3 v.a. *kill.*

interpres, -etis, m. *interpreter, expounder.*

interrogō, -āre, -āvī, -ātum, 1 v.a. *ask.*

intersum, -esse, -fuī, irreg. v.n. *be among, engage in.*

intervallum, -ī, n. *interval, distance.*

interveniō, -īre, -vēnī, -ventum, 4 v.n. *intervene.*

intolerābilis, -e, *intolerable.*

intueor, -ērī, -itus sum, 2 dep. v.a. *look at.*

inultus, -a, -um, *unavenged.*

inveniō, -īre, -vēnī, -ventum, 4 v.a. *find.*

invicem, adv. *in turn.*

invidia, -ae, f. *envy, hatred.*

invītō, -āre, -āvī, -ātum, 1 v.a. *invite.*

invocō, -āre, -āvī, -ātum, 1 v.a. *invoke.*

ipse,-a,-um,pron.*self,himself.*

īra, -ae, f. *anger.*

īrascor, -ī, īrātus sum, 3 dep. v.n. *be angry.*

is, ea, id, demonstr. pron.*that, he.*

iste, -a, -ud, demonstr. pron. *that, that by you.*

ita, adv. *thus, so, to such a degree, accordingly.*

itaque, adv. *and so, therefore, accordingly.*

iter, itineris, n.*way, journey.*

iterum, adv. *again, a second time.*

iaceō, -ēre, -cuī, 2 v.n. *lie, be prostrate.*

iaciō,iacere, iēcī,iactum,3 v.a. *throw.*

iactō, -āre, -āvī, -ātum, 1 v.a. *throw about, boast.*

iam, adv. *now, already, by this time.*

iocus, -ī, m. *joke, jest, sport.*

iubeō, -ēre, iussī, iussum, 2 v.a. *order.*

iūdicō, -āre, -āvī, -ātum, 1 v.n. *judge.*

iugulum, -ī, n. *throat.*

iungō, -ēre, -nxī, -nctum, 3 v.a. *join.*

iūs, iūris, n. *right, law, law-court.*

iussus, -ūs, m. *command.*

iustitia, -ae, f. *justice.*

iuvenis,-is, m.*youth, warrior*; comp. iūnior, *younger.*

iuventūs, -tūtis, f. *body of youths.*

iuvō, -āre, iūvī, iūtum, 1 v.a. *help.*

labor, -ōris, m. *labour.*

lacer, -a, -um, *mangled.*

lacrima, -ae, f. *tear.*
laetus, -a, -um, *glad, bountiful.*
laevus, -a, -um, *left* ; subst.
laeva, f. *left hand.*
lambō, -ere, 3 v.a. *lick.*
lapicĭda, -ae, m. *stone-cutter.*
lapideus, -a, -um, *of stone.*
lapis, -idis, m. *stone.*
lateō, -ēre, -uī, 2 v.n. *lie
hid.*
latrō, -ōnis, m. *robber.*
laus, laudis, f. *praise.*
lēgātiō, -ōnis, f. *embassy.*
lēgātus, -ī, m. *ambassador.*
legiō, -ōnis, f. *legion.*
lēgitimus, -a, -um, *lawful.*
legō, -ere, lēgī, lectum, 3 v.a.
choose.
lēniō, -īre, -īvī or iī, -ītum, 4
v.a. and n. *soften.*
lentē, adv. *slowly.*
levis, -e, *light, gentle.*
lex, lēgis, f. *law.*
līberātor, -ōris, m. *deliverer.*
līberī, -ōrum and -um, m. pl.
children.
līberō, -āre, -āvī, -ātum, 1 v.a.
liberate, set free.
lībertās, -ātis, f. *liberty.*
licet, -ēre, -uit, 2 impers. v.
it is allowed.
lictor, -ōris, m. *lictor.*
ligneus, -a, -um, *wooden.*
lignum, -ī, n. *log.*
lingua, -ae, f. *tongue.*
lituus, -ī, m. *rod.*
locō, -āre, -āvī, -ātum, 1 v.a.
place.
locus, -ī, m. *place* ; pl. locī,
m. and loca, n.
longē, adv. *far off, far.*
longus, -a, -um, *long.*
lūcus, -ī, m. *grove.*
ludibrium, -ī, n. *mockery,
laughing-stock.*
ludicrum, -ī, n. *performance.*
lūdus, -ī, m. *game.*

lūgeō, -ēre, -xī, -ctum, 2 v.a.
mourn.
lūmen, -inis, n. *light.*
lūna, -ae, f. *moon.*
lupa, -ae, f. *she-wolf.*
lux, lūcis, f. *light.*

maestus, -a, -um, *sad, mournful.*
magis, adv. *rather, more.*
magister, -trī, m. *master, chief,
teacher.*
magnitūdō, -inis, f. *greatness,
size.*
magnus, -a, -um, adj. *great* ;
māior, -us, *greater* ; maximus, -a, -um, *greatest.*
male, adv. *badly.*
mālō, malle, -uī, irreg. v.a.
prefer.
malum, -ī, n. *evil.*
malus, -a, -um, *bad, wicked.*
mandātum, -ī, n. *command.*
maneō, -ēre, mansī, mansum,
2 v.n. *remain.*
manifestus, -a, -um, *manifest.*
mānō, -āre, -āvī, -ātum, 1 v.n.
flow, spread.
manus, -ūs, f. *hand, band.*
mare, -is, n. *sea.*
māter, -tris, f. *mother.*
māteria, -ae, f. *matter, cause,
opportunity.*
mātrimōnium, -ī, n. *marriage.*
maximē, adv. *especially, most.*
maximus. See magnus.
medius, -a, -um, *middle.*
memorō, -āre, -āvī, -ātum,
1 v.a. *relate.*
mens, -ntis, f. *mind.*
mensis, -is, m. *month.*
mercēs, -ēdis, f. *reward.*
merĭdiēs, -eī, m. *noon, the
south.*
meritum, -ī, n. *desert, service.*
metuō, -ere, -uī, 3 v.a. *fear.*
metus, -ūs, m. *fear.*
meus, -a, -um, *my, mine.*

micō, -āre, -cuī, 1 v.n. *shine,
    glitter.*
migrō, -āre, -āvī, -ātum, 1 v.n.
    emigrate.
mīles, -itis, m. *soldier.*
mīlitāris, -e, *military.*
mīlitia, -ae, f. *military service.*
mille, pl. millia, *thousand.*
minimē, adv. *least.*
minister, -trī, m. *assistant.*
minor, -us, *less.*
minus, adv. *less.*
mīrābilis, -e, *wonderful.*
mīrāculum, -ī, n. *miracle.*
mīror, -ārī, -ātus sum, 1 dep.
    v.a. and n. *wonder, admire.*
mīrus, -a, -um, *wonderful.*
miseria, -ae, f. *misery, wretch-
    edness.*
mītigō, -āre, -āvī, -ātum, 1 v.a.
    assuage.
mītis, -e, *gentle.*
mittō, -ere, mīsī, missum,
    3 v.a. *send, throw.*
moderātus, -a, -um, *moderate,
    reasonable.*
modo, adv. *only ; at one time...
    at another time.*
modus, -ī, m. *manner.*
moenia, -um, n. pl. *town-walls.*
mōlēs, -is, f. *mass, bulk.*
moneō, -ēre, -uī, -itum, 2 v.a.
    warn, advise.
monitus, -ūs, m. *warning,
    advice.*
monumentum, -ī, n. *memorial,
    monument.*
mons, -ntis, m. *mountain.*
morior, morī, mortuus sum,
    3 dep. v.n. *die.*
moribundus, -a, -um, *dying.*
mors, mortis, f. *death.*
mortālis, -e, *mortal.*
mōs, mōris, m. *custom* ; pl.
    manners, character.
mōtus, -ūs, m. *movement, dis-
    turbance.*

moveō, -ēre, mōvī, mōtum,
    2 v.a. *move.*
mox, adv. *presently, soon,
    afterwards.*
mūgiō, -īre, -īvī, -ītum, 4 v.n.
    low.
mulier, -eris, f. *woman.*
multitūdo, -inis, f. *multitude,
    population.*
multus, -a, -um, *much, many.*
mūnia, pl. n. *duties.*
munīmentum, -ī, n. *fortifica-
    tion.*
mūniō, -īre, -īvī, -ītum, 4 v.a.
    fortify.
mūnītiō, -ōnis, f. *fortification.*
mūrus, -ī, m. *wall.*
mūtō, -āre, -āvī, -ātum, 1 v.a.
    change.

nam and namque, conj. *for.*
nanciscor, -ī, nactus sum,
    3 dep. v.a. *obtain.*
nascor, -ī, nātus sum, 3 dep.
    v.n. *be born.*
nātus, -ī, m. *son.*
nē, conj. *lest, that not, not.*
ne, enclitic, *whether.*
nec and neque, neg. conj.
    neither, nor.
necō, -āre, -āvī, -ātum, 1 v.a.
    kill.
nefandus, -a, -um, *unutterable,
    impious.*
negōtium, -ī, n. *business.*
nepōs, -ōtis, m. *grandson.*
nēquāquam, adv. *by no means.*
nēquīquam, adv. *in vain.*
nihil and nīl, n. *nothing.*
nimbus, -ī, m. *rain-storm, cloud.*
nisi, conj. *unless.*
nītor, -ī, nīsus or nixus sum,
    3 dep. v.n. *strive.*
nōbilitās, -ātis, f. *nobility.*
nōbilitō, -āre, -āvī, -ātum,
    1 v.a. *make famous.*
nocturnus, -a, -um, *by night.*

Vocabulary

nōlō, nolle, nōluī, irreg. v.a. and n. *be unwilling.*
nōmen, -inis, n. *name.*
nōn, neg. adv. *not.*
nondum, adv. *not yet.*
nonne, inter. neg. adv. *not?*
noscō, -ere, nōvī, nōtum, 3 v.a. *know.*
noster, -tra, -trum, poss. pron. *our.*
novācula, -ae, f. *razor.*
novus, -a, -um, *new, strange.*
nox, noctis, f. *night.*
nullus, -a, -um, *none.*
num, inter. particle, expecting a negative answer.
numerus, -ī, m. *number.*
nunc, adv. *now.*
nunquam, neg. adv. *never.*
nuntiō, -āre, -āvī, -ātum, 1 v.a. *announce.*
nuntius, -ī, m. *messenger;* plur. *news.*
nusquam, neg. adv. *nowhere.*
nutriō, -īre, -īvī, -ītum, 4 v.a. *nourish, rear.*

ō, interj. *oh!*
ob, prep. with acc. *on account of.*
obeō, -īre, -īvī or -iī, -itum, 4 v.a. and n. *perform, die.*
obiciō, -ere, -iēcī, -iectum, 3 v.a. *throw before, expose.*
oblīviscor, -ī, oblitus sum, 3 dep. v.a. *forget.*
obloquor, -ī, -locūtus sum, 3 dep. v.a. and n. *speak against.*
obnūbō, -ere, -psī, -ptum, 3 v.a. *cover.*
obruō, -ere, -uī, -utum, 3 v.a. *overwhelm.*
obstō, -āre, -stitī, 1 v.n. *oppose, counterbalance.*
obstrepō, -ere, -uī, -itum, 3 v.n. *clamour at.*
obtentus, -ūs, m. *pretext.*

obvius, -a, -um, *meeting.*
occidō, -ere, -cidī, -cāsum, 3 v.n. *fall, perish.*
occultus, -a, -um, *hidden.*
oculus, -ī, m. *eye.*
odium, -ī, n. *hatred.*
ōlim, adv. *formerly.*
omnīnō, adv. *altogether.*
omnis, -e, *all, every.*
onustus, -a, -um, *laden.*
opera, -ae, f. *work, pains;* plur. *work-people.*
operiō, -īre, -uī, -pertum, 4 v.a. *cover.*
opēs, -um, f. pl. *wealth, power.*
opifex, -icis, m. and f. *worker.*
opperior, -īrī, -pertus sum, 4 dep. v.a. *wait for.*
opportunē, adv. *opportunely, in the nick of time.*
opprimō, -ere, -pressī, -pressum, 3 v.a. *crush, surprise, overcome.*
optimus, -a, -um, superl. of bonus, *best.*
opulenter, adv. *richly.*
opus, -eris, n. *work, need.*
ōrāculum, -ī, n. *oracle.*
ōrātiō, -ōnis, f. *speech.*
orbis, -is, m. *circle, world.*
orbitās, -ātis, f. *bereavement.*
orbus, -a, -um, *bereaved.*
ordior, -īrī, orsus sum, 4 dep. v.a. *begin.*
ordō, -inis, m. *order, rank.*
orior, -īrī, ortus sum, 4 dep. v.n. *rise.*
ōrō, -āre, -āvī, -ātum, 1 v.a. *pray.*
ōs, ōris, n. *mouth.*
osculum, -ī, n. *kiss.*
ostendō, -ere, -ndī, -ntum, 3 v.a. *show.*
ōtium, -ī, n. *ease.*
ovō, -āre, -āvī, -ātum, 1 v.n. *rejoice, triumph.*

pābulum, -ī, n. *pasture.*
paene, adv. *almost.*
paenitet, -ēre, -uit, 2 impers.
　v. *it repents.*
palam, adv. *openly.*
palūdāmentum, -ī, n. *military
　cloak.*
papāver, -eris, n. *poppy.*
pār, paris, *equal.*
parcō, -ere, pepercī, parsum,
　3 v.a. *spare.*
parens, -ntis, m. and f. *parent.*
pariō, -ere, peperī, partum,
　3 v.a. *bring forth, produce.*
pariter, adv. *equally.*
parō, -āre, -āvī, -ātum, 1 v.a.
　prepare.
pars, -rtis, f. *part.*
parvus, -a, -um, *small.*
passim, adv. *in different di-
　rections.*
passus, -a, -um (pf. part. of
　pando, *spread*), *dishevelled.*
passus, -ūs, m. *pace.*
pastor, -ōris, m. *shepherd.*
pateō, -ēre, -uī, 2 v.n. *be
　open.*
pater, -tris, m. *father.*
paternus, -a, -um, *of a father,
　paternal.*
patior, patī, passus sum, 3
　dep. v.a. *endure, suffer.*
patricius, -ī, m. *patrician.*
paucī, -ae, -a, *few.*
paulisper, adv. *for a little
　while.*
paulō, adv. *by a little.*
paulum, adv. *a little.*
pavidus, -a, -um, *fearful.*
pavor, -ōris, m. *fear.*
pax, pācis, f. *peace.*
pectus, -oris, n. *breast.*
pecūnia, -ae, f. *money.*
pecus, pecoris, n. *cattle.*
penātēs, -ium, m. pl. *house-
　hold gods, home.*
pēnūria, -ae, f. *want.*

per, prep. with acc. *through.*
peragō, -ere, -ēgī, -actum,
　3 v.a. *perform, go through.*
peragrō, -āre, -āvī, -ātum,
　1 v.a. *traverse.*
peregrīnus, -a, -um, *foreign.*
pereō, -īre, -iī, -itum, 4 v.n.
　perish.
perferō, -ferre, -tulī, -lātum,
　irreg. v.a. *carry through.*
perfidia, -ae, f. *treachery.*
perficiō, -ere, fēcī, -fectum,
　3 v.a. *complete.*
perfugiō, -ere, -fūgī, -fugitum,
　3 v.n. *escape.*
perfundō, -ere, -fūdī, -fūsum,
　3 v.a. *drench, fill.*
pergō, -ere, perrexī, perrec-
　tum, 3 v.n. *proceed.*
perīculum, -ī, n. *danger.*
perītus, -a, -um, *skilled.*
perlustrō, -āre, -āvī, -ātum,
　1 v.a. *survey.*
perobscūrus, -a, -um, *very
　obscure.*
perpellō, -ere, -pulī, -pulsum,
　3 v.a. *compel, bring about.*
perstringō, -ere, -strinxī,
　-strictum, 3 v.a. *graze,
　touch, affect.*
pertineō, -ēre, -uī, 2 v.n.
　appertain.
pessimus, -a, -um (superl. of
　malus) *very bad, worst.*
petō, -ere, -īvī or -iī, -ītum,
　3 v.a. *seek.*
piget, -ēre, -uit, 2 impers. v.n.
　it irks, disgusts.
pilleus, -ī, m. *cap.*
placet, -ēre, -uit, 2 impers.
　v.n. *it pleases.*
plebs, plēbis, f. *common people.*
plērīque, pleraeque, pleraque,
　most.
plērumque, adv. *generally.*
pluit, -ere, pluit or plūvit,
　3 impers. v.n. *it rains.*

plūrimus, -a, -um (superl. of multus), *very many, most.*

plūs, gen. plūris, n. in sing. *more*; pl. m. and f. plūrēs, n. plūra, *more.*

poena, -ae, f. *penalty.*

poenitet, -ēre, -uit, 2 impers. v.n. *it repents.*

pōnō, -ere, posuī, positum, 3 v.a. *place.*

pons, pontis, m. *bridge.*

populus, -ī, m. *people.*

porrō, adv. *forward, farther on.*

porta, -ae, f. *gate.*

portendō, -ere, -ndī, -ntum, 3 v.a. *portend, presage.*

portentum, -ī, n. *portent.*

portō, -āre, -āvī, -ātum, 1 v.a. *carry.*

possum, posse, potuī, irreg. v.n. *be able.*

post, prep. with acc. *after*; adv. *after, afterwards.*

posteā, adv. *afterwards.*

posterus, -a, -um, *subsequent.*

postquam, conj. *after that.*

postrēmō, adv. *lastly.*

postulō, -āre, -āvī, -ātum, 1 v.a. *demand.*

potens, -ntis, adj. *powerful.*

potior, -īrī, -ītus sum, 4 dep. v.a. *get possession of.*

potissimus, -a, -um, superl. adj. *special, principal.*

potius, comp. adv. *rather.*

prae, prep. with abl. *in front of.*

praebeō, -ēre, -uī, -itum, 2 v.a. *afford.*

praecipiō, -ere, -cēpī, -ceptum, 3 v.a. *instruct.*

praecipuē, adv. *especially.*

praeda, -ae, f. *prey, booty.*

praeferō, -ferre, -tulī, -latum, irreg. v.a. *prefer.*

praemittō, -ere, -mīsī, -missum, 3 v.a. *send forward.*

praesens, -ntis, adj. *present.*

praesidium, -ī, n. *protection.*

praesum, -esse, -fuī, irreg. v.n. *be at the head of, command.*

praeter, prep. with acc. *except, beside.*

precem, f. def., *prayer.*

precor, -ārī, -ātus sum, 1 dep. v.a. *pray.*

pretium, -ī, n. *price.*

prīmō, adv. *at first.*

prīmōres, -um, m. *leading men.*

prīmum, adv. *first, at first.*

prīmus, -a, -um, *first.* ¦

princeps, -ipis, m. *chief man.*

principium, -ī, n. *beginning.*

prior, comp. adj. *former, first.*

priscus, -a, -um, *old-fashioned, the elder.*

priusquam, conj. *before that.*

prīvātus, -a, -um, *private.*

prō, prep. with abl. *for, in front of, in accordance with, instead of.*

prōcēdō, -ere, -cessī, -cessum, 3 v.n. *go forward.*

procella, -ae, f. *storm.*

procerēs, -um, m. *nobles.*

prōclāmō, -āre, -āvī, -ātum, 1 v.n. *proclaim.*

procul, adv. *far off.*

prōcumbō, -ere, -cubuī, -cubitum, 3 v.n. *fall down, throw oneself down.*

prōdeō, -īre, -iī, -itum, 4 v.n. *go forth.*

prōdigium, -ī, n. *prodigy.*

prōditor, -ōris, m. *traitor.*

proelium, -ī, n. *battle.*

prōferō, -ferre, -tulī, -lātum, irreg. v.a. *carry forward.*

proficiscor, -ī, -fectus sum, 3 dep. v.n. *set out.*

prōfluō, -ere, -fluxī, -fluxum, 3 v.n. *flow forth, flow.*

prŏfŭgiŏ, -ere, -fūgī, -fugitum, 3 v.n. *flee forth.*

progeniēs, -eī, f. *offspring.*

prohibeŏ, -ere, -uī, -itum, 2 v.a. *hinder.*

proinde, adv. *therefore, accordingly.*

prŏlābor, -ī, -lapsus sum, 3 dep. v.n. *fall forward.*

promptus, -a, -um, *ready.*

prope, adv. *near, nearly*; prep. with acc. *near.*

properē, adv. *hastily.*

properŏ, -āre, -āvī, -ātum, 1 v.n. *hasten.*

propinquus, -a, -um, *neighbouring, related.*

propitius, -a, -um, *propitious, favourable.*

propter, prep. with acc. *on account of.*

prŏvocātiŏ, -ōnis, f. *appeal.*

prŏvocŏ, -āre, -āvī, -ātum, 1 v.n. *appeal.*

proximus, superl. adj. *nearest, most recent.*

pūbēs, -is, f. *body of youths.*

pūblicus, -a, -um, *public.*

puer, -ī, m. *boy, child.*

puerīlis, -e, *childish.*

pugna, -ae, f. *battle, fight.*

pugnŏ, -āre, -āvī, -ātum, 1 v.n. *fight.*

pulchritūdŏ, -inis, f. *beauty.*

putŏ, -āre, -āvī, -ātum, 1 v.a. and n. *think.*

quā, adv. *where.*

quadrāgintā, indecl. *forty.*

quadrīgae, -ārum, f. *four-horse team, chariot.*

quadringentī, -ae, -a, *four hundred.*

quaerŏ, -ere, quaesīvī, quaesītum, 3 v.a. *seek, enquire.*

quam, conj. *than.*

quattuor, indecl. *four.*

que, enclitic conj. *both, and.*

querella, -ae, f. *complaint.*

queror, -ī, questus sum, 3 dep. v.n. *complain.*

quī, quae, quod, rel. pron. *who, which.*

quīcumque, quaecumque, quodcumque, rel. pron. *whoever.*

quīdam, quaedam, quoddam, indef. pron. *a certain one, certain.*

quiēs, -ētis, f. *rest.*

quiescŏ, -ere, -ēvī, -ētum, 3 v.n. *remain quiet.*

quīlibet, quaelibet, quodlibet and quidlibet, indef. pron. *anyone you please.*

quinque, indecl. *five.*

quis or **quī**, qua or quae, quid or quod, (1) inter. pron. *who? what?* (2) indef. pron. *anyone, anything.*

quisnam, quaenam, quodnam or quidnam, inter. pron. *who then?*

quisque, quaeque, quidque, indef. pron. *each.*

quŏ, (1) adv. *whither*; (2) conj. *in order that.*

quod, conj. *because.*

quoniam, conj. *since.*

quoque, conj. *also.*

rapiŏ, -ere, rapuī, raptum, 3 v.a. *seize.*

ratiŏ, -ōnis, f. *reason, plan, method.*

rebellŏ, -āre, -āvī, -ātum, 1 v.n. *renew war, rebel.*

recens, -ntis, adj. *fresh, recent.*

recenseŏ, -ēre, -uī, -um, 2 v.a. *review.*

recipiŏ, -ere, -cēpī, -ceptum, 3 v.a. *receive, betake.*

reddŏ, -dere, -didī, -ditum, 3 v.a. *give back, return, render.*

redeō, -īre, -īvī or -iī, -itum, irreg. v.n. *return.*

redūcō, -ere, -xī, -ctum, 3 v.a. *lead back.*

referō, -ferre, rettulī, relātum, irreg. v.a. *bring back, relate.*

reficiō, -ere, -fēcī, -fectum, 3 v.a. *restore, refresh.*

rēgia, -ae, f. *palace.*

rēgīna, -ae, f. *queen.*

rēgius, -a, -um, *royal.*

regnō, -āre, -āvī, -ātum, 1 v.n. *reign.*

regnum, -ī, n. *kingdom.*

regō, -ere, rexī, rectum, 3 v.a. *rule.*

religiō, -ōnis, f. *conscientiousness, religious feeling.*

relinquō, -ere, -līquī, -lictum, 3 v.a. *leave behind.*

reor, ratus sum, 2 dep. v.n. *think.*

repentē, adv. *suddenly.*

repentīnus, -a, -um, *sudden, upstart.*

repetō, -ere, -īvī or -iī, -ītum, 3 v.a. *seek to recover.*

repōnō, -ere, -posuī, -positum, 3 v.a. *replace.*

reputō, -āre, -āvī, -ātum, 1 v.a. *think over.*

rēs, reī, f. *thing, affair, property, state*; **res pūblica**, *commonwealth, government, state.*

reservō, -āre, -āvī, -ātum, 1 v.a. *reserve.*

resistō, -ere, restitī, 3 v.n. *stand still, resist.*

respergō, -ere, -spersī, -spersum, 3 v.a. *sprinkle.*

respiciō, -ere, -spexī, -spectum, 3 v.a. *look back, regard.*

respondeō, -ēre, -ndī, -nsum, 2 v.a. and n. *answer.*

responsum, -ī, n. *answer.*

restinguō, -ere, -nxī, -nctum, 3 v.a. *quench.*

retineō, -ēre, -uī, -tentum, 2 v.a. *hold back, retain.*

retrō, adv. *backwards.*

revehō, -ere, -vexī, -vectum, 3 v.a. *carry back.*

rex, rēgis, m. *king.*

rīpa, -ae, f. *bank.*

rītus, -ūs, m. *rite.*

rixa, -ae, f. *quarrel, brawl.*

rōbur, -oris, n. *oak, strength.*

rogitō, -āre, -āvī, -ātum, 1 v.a. *keep asking, ask eagerly.*

rogō, -āre, -āvī, -ātum, 1 v.a. *ask.*

ruīna, -ae, f. *downfall, ruin.*

ruō, -ere, ruī, 3 v.n. *fall down, rush.*

sacerdōs, -dōtis, m. and f. *priest, priestess.*

sacellum, -ī, n. *shrine, chapel.*

sacra, -ōrum, n. pl. *sacred rites, sacrifices.*

saepe, adv. *often.*

saepiō, -īre, saepsī, saeptum, 4 v.a. *enclose.*

saevitia, -ae, f. *savagery, cruelty.*

salīnae, -ārum, f. *salt-works.*

saltus, -ūs, m. *forest, woodland, valley.*

salūbris, -e, *healthy.*

salūtō, -āre, -āvī, -ātum, 1 v.a. *salute.*

salveō, -ēre, 2 v.n. *be in good health.*

sanctus, -a, -um, *holy.*

sanguis, -inis, m. *blood.*

satis, adv. *enough, sufficiently.*

scelerātus, -a, -um, *wicked, criminal.*

scelus, -eris, n. *crime, wickedness.*

scīlicet, adv. *in truth, forsooth.*

sciō, scīre, scīvī, scītum, 4 v.a. and n. *know.*

sciscitor, -ārī, -ātus sum, 1 dep. v.a. and n. *enquire.*

scūtum, -ī, n. *shield.*

sē and sēsē, suī, reflexive pron. *himself.*

sēcrētum, -ī, n. *a place apart, privacy.*

secundus, -a, -um, *second.*

secūris, -is, f. *axe.*

sed, conj. *but.*

sedeō, -ēre, sēdī, sessum, 2 v.n. *sit.*

sēdō, -āre, -āvī, -ātum, 1 v.a. *settle, calm.*

sēdes, -is, f. *seat.*

sēgregō, -āre, -āvī, -ātum, 1 v.a. *separate.*

sella, -ae, f. *chair.*

semper, adv. *always.*

senātor, -ōris, m. *senator.*

senātus, -ūs, m. *senate.*

senescō, -ere, -nuī, 3 v.n. *grow old.*

senex, -nis, *old.*

sensim, adv. *perceptibly, gradually.*

sensus, -ūs, m. *feeling, sense.*

sentiō, -īre, -nsī, -nsum, 4 v.a. and n. *feel.*

sepeliō, -īre, -īvī, sepultum, 4 v.a. *bury.*

septem, indecl. *seven.*

sepulcrum, -ī, n. *sepulchre.*

sepultūra, -ae, f. *burial.*

sequor, -ī, secūtus sum, 3 dep. v.a. *follow.*

serēnus, -a, -um, *clear, fine.*

sēria, -ōrum, n. pl. *serious tasks.*

serva, -ae, f. *female slave.*

serviō, -īre, -īvī or -iī, -ītum, 4 v.n. *be a slave.*

servitium, -ī, n. *slavery.*

servō, -āre, -āvī, -ātum, 1 v.a. *keep, preserve.*

servus, -ī, m. *slave.*

sex, indecl. *six.*

sī, conj. *if.*

sīc, adv. *so, thus.*

siccum, -ī, n. *dry land.*

sīcut, adv. *just as.*

signum, -ī, n. *sign.*

sileō, -ēre, -uī, 2 v.n. *be silent.*

silva, -ae, f. *wood, forest.*

similis, -e, *like.*

simul, adv. *at the same time.*

simulātiō, -ōnis, f. *pretence.*

simulō, -āre, -āvī, -ātum, 1 v.a. *pretend.*

simultas, -ātis, f. *quarrel.*

sine, prep. with abl. *without.*

singulus, -a, -um, *one each, single.*

sinister, -tra, -trum, *left.*

sinō, -ere, sīvī, 3 v.a. *allow.*

sitiens, -entis, *thirsty.*

situs, -a, -um, *placed, situate.*

socer, -erī, m. *father-in-law.*

societās, -ātis, f. *alliance.*

socius, -ī, m. *ally.*

soleō, -ēre, -itus sum, 2 semi-dep. v.n. *be accustomed.*

sollemnis, -e, *solemn, sacred.*

sollicitus, -a, -um, *troubled.*

sōlum, adv. *only.*

solum, -ī, n. *soil, ground.*

sōlus, -a, -um, *alone.*

solvō, -ere, -vī, solūtum, 3 v.a. *loosen, break up.*

somnus, -ī, m. *sleep.*

sōpiō, -īre, -īvī, -ītum, 4 v.a. *send to sleep, stun.*

sopor, -ōris, m. *sleep.*

sordidus, -a, -um, *soiled, shabby.*

soror, -ōris, f. *sister.*

sors, sortis, f. *lot.*

sospitō, -āre, -āvī, -ātum, 1 v.a. *keep safe.*

spatium, -ī, n. *space, distance.*

species, -eī, f. *appearance, guise.*

spectāculum, -ī, n. *spectacle.*

spectō, -āre, -āvī, -ātum, 1 v.a. *look, look at*; part. **spectātus,** -a, -um, *tested, proved.*

specus, -ūs, m. *cave.*

spēlunca, -ae, f. *cave.*

spernō, -ere, sprēvī, sprētum, 3 v.a. *despise.*

spērō, -āre, -āvī, -ātum, 1 v.n. and a. *hope.*

spēs, -eī, f. *hope.*

spīritus, -ūs, m. *breath.*

spoliō, -āre, -āvī, -ātum, 1 v.a. *spoil, strip.*

spolium, -ī, n. *spoil.*

sponsus, -ī, m. *betrothed.*

sponte, only abl. sing. f. *free will.*

statim, adv. *immediately.*

statua, -ae, f. *statue.*

statuō, -ere, -uī, -ūtum, 3 v.a. *set up, determine.*

stimulō, -āre, -āvī, -ātum, 1 v.a. *goad, excite.*

stirps, stirpis, f. *stock, family.*

stō, stāre, stetī, statum, 1 v.n. *stand.*

strāges, -is, f. *destruction, slaughter.*

strēnuus, -a, -um, *active, strenuous.*

stringō, -ere, -nxī, -ctum, 3 v.a. *draw.*

studium, -ī, n. *zeal.*

stultitia, -ae, f. *folly, stupidity.*

sub, prep. with acc. and abl. *under.*

subiciō, -ere, -iēcī, -iectum, 3 v.a. *throw under, place under.*

subitō, adv. *suddenly.*

subitus, -a, -um, *sudden.*

sublica, -ae, f. *stake, pile.*

sublīmis, -e, *high, aloft.*

succēdō, -ere, -cessī, -cessum, 3 v.n. *come under, come next, succeed.*

sum, esse, fuī, irreg. v.n. *be.*

summus, -a, -um (superl. of superus), *highest.*

sumō, -ere, -mpsī, -mptum, 3 v.a. *take.*

super, prep. with acc. *above, over.*

superbia, -ae, f. *pride, arrogance.*

superbus, -a, -um, *proud, arrogant, tyrannical*; adv. **superbē,** *proudly.*

superior, -us (comp. of superus), *higher, superior, former.*

supersum, -esse, -fuī, irreg. v.n. *be over and above, be left, survive.*

supplicium, -ī, n. *punishment, execution.*

suspendō, -ere, -dī, -sum, 3 v.a. *hang up, suspend*; pf. part. **suspensus,** *in suspense.*

sustineō, -ēre, -tinuī, -tentum, 2 v.a. *bear up, sustain, check.*

suus, -a, -um, reflexive poss. pron. *his own.*

tacitus, -a, -um, *silent.*

taedet, -ēre, 2 v. impers. *it disgusts, it wearies.*

tālis, -e, *such.*

tam, adv. *so.*

tamen, adv. *nevertheless, however.*

tandem, adv. *at length.*

tanquam, adv. *just as, as if.*

tantum, adv. *only.*

tantus, -a, -um, *so great.*

tectum, -ī, n. *roof, house.*

tegō, -ere, texī, tectum, 3 v.a. *cover.*

tēlum, -ī, n. *weapon.*

temperō, -āre, -āvī, -ātum, 1 v.n. *refrain from, spare.*

tempestās, -ātis, f. *storm.*

templum, -ī, n. *quarter, circuit, temple.*

tempus, -oris, n. *time.*

teneō, -ēre, -nuī, -ntum, 2 v.a. *hold;* v.n. *prevail.*

tenuis, -e, *thin, shallow.*

tergum, -ī, n. *back, rear.*

ternī, -ae, -a, *three each.*

terra, -ae, f. *land, earth.*

terribilis, -e, *terrible.*

tertius, -a, -um, *third.*

testāmentum, -ī, n. *will.*

tollō, -ere, sustulī, sublātum, 3 v.a. *lift up, remove, destroy.*

tonitrus, -ūs, m. *thunder.*

torpeō, -ēre, -uī, 2 v.n. *be numb, be torpid.*

tōtus, -a, -um, *whole.*

trabea, -ae, f. *striped robe of state.*

trādō, -ere, -didī, -ditum, 3 v.a. *give up, hand on, relate.*

trādūcō, -ere, -xī, -ctum, 3 v.a. *lead across.*

trahō, -ere, traxī, tractum, 3 v.a. *drag.*

tranquillus, -a, -um, *quiet, tranquil.*

transeō, -īre, -iī, -itum, 4 v.n. *cross.*

transferō, -ferre, -tulī, -latum, irreg. v.a. *bear across.*

transfīgō, -ere, -xī, -xum, 3 v.a. *pierce through, transfix.*

transfugiō, -ere, -fūgī, -fugitum, 3 v.n. *flee across, desert.*

transiliō, -īre, -uī, 4 v.a. *leap over.*

trepidō, -āre, -āvī, -ātum, 1 v.n. *hurry, be agitated.*

trepidus, -a, -um, *restless, agitated.*

trigeminus, -a, -um, *threefold, triplet, born three at a birth.*

trīgintā, indecl. *thirty.*

triumphō, -āre, -āvī, -ātum, 1 v.n. *triumph.*

trucīdō, -āre, -āvī, -ātum, 1 v.a. *butcher, massacre.*

tum and tunc, adv. *then.*

tumultuōsē, adv. *tumultuously, in confusion.*

tumultus, -ūs, m. *uproar, tumult.*

turba, -ae, f. *crowd.*

turbō, -āre, -āvī, -ātum, 1 v.a. *disturb.*

tūtēla, -ae, f. *care, guardianship.*

tūtor, -ōris, m. *guardian.*

tūtus, -a, -um, *safe.*

ubī or ubi, adv. *where, when.*

ullus, -a, -um, *anyone, any.*

ultimus, -a, -um, *farthest, uttermost, last.*

ultor, -ōris, m. *avenger.*

ultrō, adv. *beyond, of one's own accord, unasked.*

unde, adv. *whence.*

undique, adv. *on all sides.*

unus, -a, -um, *one, only.*

urbānus, -a, -um, *of the city, urban.*

urbs, urbis, f. *city.*

usque, adv. *right on, as far as, continually.*

ut or utī, conj. *in order that, so that, when, as.*

uter, -tra, -trum, inter. pron. *which of two.*

uterque, utraque, utrumque, *each of two, both.*

ūtilis, -e, *useful.*

ūtor, -ī, usus sum, 3 dep. v.a. *use.*

utrimque, adv. *on both sides.*

uxor, -ōris, f. *wife.*

vacuus, -a, -um, *empty.*

vāgītus, -ūs, m. *squalling.*

valeō, -ēre, -uī, 2 v.n. *be strong, be well.*

validus, -a, -um, *strong.*

vānus, -a, -um, *vain, useless.*

vastō, -āre, -āvī, -ātum, 1 v.a. *devastate.*

vātēs, -is, m. *soothsayer, prophet, poet.*

vel, conj. *either, or.*

vēlō, -āre, -āvī, -ātum, 1 v.a. *veil, cover.*

velut, adv. *even as, just as.*

venerābundus, -a, -um, *venerating, reverential.*

veniō, -īre, vēnī, ventum, 4 v.n. *come.*

vēnor, -ārī, -ātus sum, 1 dep. v.a. and n. *hunt.*

ventus, -ī, m. *wind.*

verber, -eris, n. *lash, stripe.*

verberō, -āre, -āvī, -ātum, 1 v.a. *scourge, flog.*

vērē, adv. *truly.*

vertō, -ere, -rtī, -rsum, 3 v.a. *turn.*

vestibulum, -ī, n. *fore-court, portico.*

vestīgium, -ī, n. *footstep.*

vestis, -is, f. *clothes.*

vetō, -āre, -uī, -itum, 1 v.a. *forbid.*

vetus, -eris, adj. *old, ancient.*

via, -ae, f. *way, road.*

vīcīnus, -a, -um, *neighbouring.*

victor, -ōris, m. *conqueror.*

victōria, -ae, f. *victory.*

vīcus, -ī, m. *street.*

videō, -ēre, vīdī, vīsum, 2 v.a. *see.*

viduus, -a, -um, *widowed.*

vīgintī, indecl. *twenty.*

vinciō, -īre, vinxī, vinctum, 4 v.a. *bind.*

vincō, -ere, vīcī, victum, 3 v.a. *conquer.*

vindicō,-āre,-āvī,-ātum, 1 v.a. *claim.*

vīnum, -ī, n. *wine.*

violō, -āre, -āvī, -ātum, 1 v.a. *violate, harm.*

vir, virī, m. *man, husband.*

virtūs, -ūtis, f. *virtue, valour.*

vīs, vī, vim, f. *force, strength, quantity;* pl. vīrēs, vīrium, *strength.*

vīsus, -ūs, m. *sight.*

vīta, -ae, f. *life.*

vitium, -ī, n. *vice, fault.*

vīvō, -ēre, vixī, victum, 3 v.n. *live.*

vix, adv. *scarcely.*

vōciferor, -ārī, -ātus sum, 1 dep. v.n. *cry out, shout.*

vocō, -āre, -āvī, -ātum, 1 v.a. *call.*

volitō, -āre, -āvī, -ātum, 1 v.n. *fly about, flutter.*

volō, velle, voluī, irreg. v.a. and n. *wish, be willing.*

volō,-āre,-āvī,-ātum,1 v.n. *fly.*

vox, vōcis, f. *voice.*

vulgō, adv. *commonly, generally.*

vulgus, -ī, n. *common people.*

vulnerō, -āre, -āvī, -ātum, 1 v.a. *wound.*

vulnus, -eris, n. *wound.*

vultur, -uris, m. *vulture.*

vultus, -ūs, m. *countenance, look.*

INDEX OF PROPER NAMES.

The references are to pages.

CAMBRIDGE: PRINTED BY JOHN CLAY, M.A. AT THE UNIVERSITY PRESS